# THE MONEY DOCTOR

# THE MONEY DOCTOR

## How to achieve total financial health — quickly and easily

John Lowe

Gill & Macmillan

Gill & Macmillan Ltd
Hume Avenue, Park West, Dublin 12
with associated companies throughout the world
www.gillmacmillan.ie
© John Lowe 2004

ISBN-13: 978 07171 3822 7
ISBN-10: 0 7171 3822 4
Index compiled by Grainne Farren
Print origination by TypeIT, Dublin
Printed by ColourBooks Ltd, Dublin

This book is typeset in 12 Adobe Garamond on 15pt.

*The paper used in this book comes from the wood pulp of managed forests.*
*For every tree felled, at least one tree is planted,*
*thereby renewing natural resources.*

A CIP catalogue record for this book is available from the
British Library.

5 7 8 6 4

Whilst every effort has been made to ensure accuracy, no legal or
other liability on the part of the author or publishers can be
accepted for any information or advice given.

# CONTENTS

Acknowledgments                                    viii

Preface                                              ix

Is this book for you?                                xi

Getting the most out of this book                   xii

Visit the Money Doctor web site                     xiv


PART ONE
THE PRINCIPLES OF FINANCIAL HEALTH

1.  Getting on with your money — how to have the
    perfect relationship with your money            3

2.  Learn to speak the language — a quick guide
    to the most important personal finance
    terminology (see also Jargon Buster at the back
    of this book)                                    16

3.  A first-class plan — how to solve all your
    financial worries, save yourself time and make
    yourself substantially richer                    26

4.  How to write a money plan — the only way to
    guarantee your financial dreams come true        32

5.  Money is a family affair — how families can
    work together to achieve long-term financial
    security                                         56

6.  Financial products made easy — a quick
    introduction to all the financial products you
    are ever likely to want ... or need                          67

7.  Getting help — who you can really trust to give
    you the best possible advice                                 76

8.  The joy of being debt-free — why it is important
    to be debt-free PLUS how to pay off all your
    debts, including your mortgage, quickly and
    easily                                                       90

PART TWO
THE PRACTICALITIES OF FINANCIAL HEALTH

9.  Everything you need to know about mortgages
    — how to cut the cost of your home loan, plus
    answers to all your mortgage questions                       107

10. Better borrowing — a comprehensive guide
    to borrowing, from credit cards to credit
    unions                                                       130

11. Protecting yourself and your family — arranging
    the best medical, income and life cover at the
    lowest possible price                                        139

12. Protecting your possessions and other assets —
    inside tips on keeping the cost of your general
    insurance to a bare minimum                                  150

13. Retire early ... retire rich — with a small
    amount of planning and the benefit of some
    huge tax breaks, it is possible to make all your
    retirement dreams come true                                  157

14. Creating your own safety net — the quickest, most efficient way to build up an emergency fund   179

15. The science of building wealth — proven investment techniques that are guaranteed to succeed   184

16. A quick guide to saving tax — an easy-to-understand and logical approach to cutting your tax bill   201

Jargon Buster   207

Appendix 1
The Money Doctor's Annual House Budget   219

Appendix 2
The Money Doctor's Fact Find   220

Appendix 3
A typical 'Terms of Business'   232

Index   236

# ACKNOWLEDGMENTS

This seems an ideal opportunity to thank all the many people who have helped and guided me throughout my career — my family, friends, mentors and colleagues.

I would specifically like to thank the following for their assistance in the production of this book

- My family who allowed me time and space and gave great encouragement
- Jonathan Self (writer and novelist)
- George Butler (Providence Finance Services)
- Eunan King (NCB Senior Economist)
- Lucy Freeman (editor)
- Shane Hillan (Providence Finance Services)
- My colleagues in Providence Finance Services who supported me every step of the way
- Monica McInerney (novelist) for her introduction to my publishers Gill & Macmillan
- Fergal Tobin (Gill & Macmillan) and all the talented team in G&M.

# PREFACE

Why the Money Doctor? The short answer is that I aim to do for your wealth what a good doctor will do for your health. That is to say, I will show you how to overcome any financial 'illnesses' you may be suffering from and how to dramatically improve your financial fitness. You won't need to go to the pharmaceutical company directly as there are so many and you'd never know which one is for you and your 'ailment'. I don't want to stretch the analogy too far … but you can rely on me — as you would rely on a good doctor — to be honest, trustworthy and professional.

That's the short answer. Now let me give you the slightly longer answer.

In 1999, at the age of 47, I decided to resign from my job as the senior commercial lending manager of an Irish bank and turned my back on 27 years of working for mainstream financial institutions. I gave up job security, a company car and five weeks a year paid holiday. This wasn't the act of a madman, but the act of someone who had had enough of 'selling' and wanted to start 'telling'.

There is a lot right with our financial services sector. It is stable, well-regulated and offers both choice and value. But the sector has one major flaw: it is sales driven, not solution driven. Banks, building societies and insurance companies always promote their own products rather than someone else's — even if their products are less appropriate and/or more expensive. This has led to a great deal of consumer cynicism and, quite frankly, suspicion. The reason why I decided to change direction was because I wanted to be above such suspicion. I wanted to be independent — free to do what was best for the 'patient'.

With this book, and the recently launched Money Doctor web site, I aim to fill what I perceive to be a real gap in the market. That is to say, there is a real demand for:

- Reliable, up-to-date and accurate personal finance information;
- Unbiased, easy-to-understand and relevant financial advice; and
- Transparent, honest and professional service.

In particular, I have tried to cover both the principles of better financial management and the practical aspects of taking financial decisions. *The Money Doctor* will answer your questions about how to make the most of your money. If there is something you feel I have left out please let me know so that I can include it in future editions.

One final point. Dealing with money should be a pleasure, not a chore. Whether you read this book from cover to cover or dip in and out, I hope it will inspire and enthuse you.


John Lowe
Dublin, Ireland
August 2004

# IS THIS BOOK FOR YOU?

**The Money Doctor says this book will be of relevance to you if ...**

- You have money questions and don't know who to turn to for an honest, accurate, unbiased answer.
- You worry about money.
- You have, or plan to get, a mortgage.
- You have credit cards, store cards, hire purchase agreements, an overdraft, personal loans, a mortgage or any other borrowings, because you will learn how it is possible to pay all these debts off in a matter of years just by following a simple, proven, logical plan.
- You have money on deposit or save money on a regular basis.
- You want to build up your capital worth and guarantee yourself a comfortable (and possibly early) retirement.
- You have capital and don't know how to invest it.
- You want to slash your tax bill.
- You have dependents and you are worried about their well-being.
- You have (or think you should have) either life or critical illness cover.
- You are worried about the quality of financial advice you are receiving.
- You are interested in your personal relationship with money.
- You would like to know more about how consumers are being exploited by financial service companies.
- You have children.

# GETTING THE MOST OUT OF THIS BOOK

- You will find this book relevant regardless of your financial position, age or gender.

- If there is a particular subject you want to learn about then check the contents page or turn to the index.

- The book is written in plain English and contains plenty of:

  – Case histories

  – Checklists

  – Action-orientated advice

- One of the most important aspects of the guide is that it concentrates on 'how to' information, as in how to cut the cost of your mortgage, how to get rid of your debts, how to build up savings, how to save tax and how to protect your family.

- The first part of this book deals with the principles of good money management. It explores subjects such as your relationship with money, setting financial objectives, writing a money plan, and paying off all your debts including your mortgage. It also contains a description of the most relevant financial terminology and provides a quick guide to the principal types of financial product. Unlike any other book on the subject in Ireland (or indeed any other book I have been able to find), it considers topics such as teaching children about money, money and relationships and core beliefs in relation to money.

- The second part of the book concentrates on practical issues. Essentially it answers every conceivable question you could ask about mortgages, borrowing, pensions, life cover, other types of insurance, investment and tax. You'll find that the second part of the book doesn't go into any detail regarding, say, interest rates or other time-related information. Instead, all this information is available on the Money Doctor web site (*www.moneydoctor.ie*). At the end of the second part you'll find all sorts of additional information.

- Each chapter begins with a summary and ends with a list of action points.

- MONEY DOCTOR WEALTH WARNING This symbol is used to warn you about something that may have an adverse affect on your financial wealth.

- MONEY DOCTOR WEALTH CHECK This symbol is used to highlight something that could really improve your financial fitness.

# VISIT THE MONEY DOCTOR
# WEB SITE

The Money Doctor is not just a book, it is a complete service. The Money Doctor web site offers you:

- Extra articles and checklists covering a huge range of personal finance topics.

- The latest personal finance tips, advice and information.

- 100 top tax tips.

- Up-to-the-minute mortgage and investment rates.

- Special calculators allowing you to see (at the press of a button) what your mortgage or other loan will cost you — as well as how much your savings will earn you.

- An online monthly budget planner.

- Timely information such as the current tax credits and allowances.

- The chance to receive a free consultation with the Money Doctor.

- An opportunity to receive the Money Doctor's free monthly newsletter.

The web site is updated daily and all the information it contains is available without charge.

www.moneydoctor.ie

# PART ONE

# THE PRINCIPLES
# OF FINANCIAL HEALTH

# 1

## GETTING ON WITH YOUR MONEY

### HOW TO HAVE THE PERFECT RELATIONSHIP WITH YOUR MONEY

This chapter is all about how to develop a perfect relationship with money. It will be of particular interest if you fall into one of the following categories:

- You know, in your heart of hearts, that you should be spending more time sorting out your personal finances, but somehow you just haven't got around to it;
- You have — or have had — money worries (other than those caused by something beyond your control);
- You want the motivation to get to grips with your personal finances; or
- You would like to be more consistent about money.

Putting your finances on to a stronger footing can be achieved quickly and easily (as you will learn in later chapters) but to keep them there often requires a change in attitude and approach. This chapter will show you how to achieve that change.

### Your money or your life

I find it fascinating that so little gets written about human behaviour as it relates to money. It is not a subject which either psychologists or personal finance experts seem to consider important. Yet your relationship with money may affect the entire course of your life.

Let me give you a real-life example. When I met Gerry, an ex-banker, he told me that he had spent more time choosing his last car than choosing his mortgage! As a result he was, without realising it, paying one percent above the home loan market rate. He had also allowed himself to be 'sold' a very expensive life insurance plan. I calculated that, over the twenty-five-year term of Gerry's €210,000 mortgage, these two products alone would cost him a staggering additional €38,000 in unnecessary loan and insurance payments. Gerry's financial objective was to retire early. To increase his pension fund by the €38,000 he was wasting, he would have had to work for an additional three years. In other words, Gerry's relationship with money was effectively forcing him either to postpone his retirement by three years, or retire with less capital.

Gerry's behaviour is by no means unique. As the Money Doctor, I spend every day talking to intelligent, rational, sensible people who, for one reason or another, haven't been paying proper attention to their personal finances. Nine times out of ten they don't even realise what they are doing, or not doing. Without questioning it they will, amongst other things:

- Accept lower rates of return on their savings;
- Pay more tax than they have to;
- Pay more to borrow than they have to;
- Take out insurance policies they don't need or that don't necessarily provide them with the protection they want, and which are frequently over-priced;
- Make poor investment decisions;
- Fail to plan properly for their retirement; and
- Put their money at risk.

The price for neglecting their money in this way may be

much, much higher than they realise. It isn't so much the loss in any one area (though this can be extremely high as Gerry's situation reveals) as the cumulative loss arising from a string of ill-advised financial decisions. A cost that has to be measured not just in euros, but in lost opportunities since wasted money, whatever the reason, means:

- Genuine sacrifices;
- Worry and anxiety;
- Working harder and/or working for a longer period; and
- Less leisure time and fewer holidays.

If you think you might be in this position — take heart. Firstly, you are by no means alone. From my experience, I would say that nine out of ten people could dramatically improve their overall wealth with a relatively modest amount of financial planning. Secondly, sorting it out is much easier, and much less painful, than you may imagine.

## Why money makes people behave strangely

So what is it about financial decision-making that causes otherwise astute individuals to literally throw away their money?

I think there are several forces at play here. To begin with, many people are afraid of money. They are afraid of not having enough, of not using it to their best advantage, and, in a worst-case scenario, of losing it. Even those who aren't afraid may still not be entirely confident with money. How often do you hear people say 'I am embarrassed to talk about money'? There is less of a taboo talking about death than there is about money. I am sure that, at a subconscious level, fear has a great deal to do with irrational financial decision-making.

People are confused by money, too. It is possible to complete sixteen years of education in Ireland without anyone attempting to teach you money 'basics'. This is something that most financial institutions have not hesitated to turn to their advantage. Look at the small print or jargon used when describing and selling financial products. Anyone could be excused for throwing their arms up in despair.

Nor must one forget that most people deal with money issues as one-off events. When they buy a home they look for a mortgage. When they have a little extra cash they look for a savings plan. When they reach middle age they start to think about a pension. This results in a compartmentalised approach to money which, in turn, means that the bigger picture is ignored. By bigger picture I don't just mean people's overall financial well-being, I mean their whole attitude and approach to money.

## It all comes down to belief patterns

I am far too practical a person to be taken in by psycho-babble. However, I do believe that *if you want to be financially better off than you are at the moment then you simply must come to grips with your own belief patterns as they relate to money.* One method of explaining what I mean is to quote some of the different things people have said to me about money:

'I would always shop around for a better deal on most things — but not on financial products.'

'I hate talking about money. I find it embarrassing.'

'Money seems to slip through my fingers.'

'I worry about money all the time but I don't do anything about it, because I am not sure what to do.'

'Money is boring. We have enough. Why think about it?'

In my experience almost everyone has deeply-held beliefs in relation to money — usually negative beliefs. Most can be attributed to one or more of the following factors:

- *Formative experiences.* Take, for instance, the case of someone whose family suffered financial hardship when they were growing up; naturally, this would influence their attitude to money.
- *Parental influence.* Some parents talk about money, others don't — but either way children can end up being worried about there not being enough. By the same token, some parents are spendthrift whilst others are positively tight-fisted — again influencing their children's beliefs.
- *Lack of education.* Though there have been recent moves to change the national curriculum, personal finance is still not taught properly in our schools.
- *The mystification of money.* Financial institutions seem to conspire to make money as mysterious a subject as possible.
- *Lack of trust in personal finance professionals.* Bank managers are viewed as fair-weather friends and the institutions they work for as impersonal and greedy. Insurance and pensions salesmen are hardly revered in society. People are suspicious of the experts they rely on to give them advice.
- *Society's attitude to money.* There are some societies where money is openly discussed. In Ireland, however, it is considered rude to talk about money and crass to spend too much time managing it.

## The link between belief and behaviour

There is no doubt in my mind that there is a direct link between a) what you believe about money; b) your behaviour in relation to money; and c) how much money you end up having.

The fact is that if you view money in a negative way you are reducing your chances of a financially stable life. You aren't giving yourself a proper chance.

What's more, if you think that sorting out your personal finances will take more time and effort than *not* sorting them out, think again. Not paying attention to money is likely to result in you:

- Wasting a vast amount of energy worrying;
- Wasting a vast amount of cash;
- Putting yourself and your dependents at risk;
- Reducing your standard of living;
- Lengthening the number of years you have to work; and
- Suffering a shortfall in your pension fund when you reach retirement age.

If you start to think positively about money, I guarantee that you will begin to behave more positively about money. And if you *behave* more positively about money, I guarantee that you will find yourself able to build up much greater wealth.

## Start by assessing your own situation

The first step to making sure that you think positively about money is to assess your current attitude. These questions may assist you:

- Do you ever worry about money?

- Does your heart sink when you have to think about money?
- Do you ever wish you hadn't made particular purchases?
- Do you ever indulge in 'retail therapy' or 'comfort spending' — buying things you don't really want or need?
- Have you taken on more debt than you can comfortably manage?
- Are you worried about earning enough money for your needs?
- Do you hide the amount of money you have (or the size of your debts) from yourself or other people?
- Do you feel guilty when you have money?

If you have answered 'yes' to any of these questions I'd like to suggest that you spend a little time contemplating why you feel the way you do. It may help to consider some of the following subjects:

- Your parents' attitude to money.
- Any important experiences you may have had in relation to money.
- Good money habits you believe you have.
- Bad money habits you believe you have.
- Whether there is anyone you trust to help you with your personal finances — and if there is, why you trust them.
- What aspects of personal finance you feel confident about.
- What aspects of personal finance worry or confuse you.
- How you would like to change your relationship with money.

Doing this may strike you as being a waste of time to begin with. But unravelling your personal money history in this way is crucial if you want to instigate lasting changes.

## On the Money Doctor's couch

Here are some of the things my 'patients' have told me about their relationship to money.

'My father was very careless with money and my mother was always struggling to feed and clothe us. She did a wonderful job but by the time I was an adult I was fed up with the constant scrimping and saving. As a reaction to this I became just like my father. I spent every penny I earned, and then some, and never saved.'

'I come from an extremely cautious background. No one in my family liked to take risks or do anything which would ever get us noticed. I was taught never to question people in authority or to complain. I saved all my life, but I never invested it very wisely. I just accepted what I was told by whoever was advising me. I didn't challenge anything anyone said.'

'I have always rushed into every financial decision, never stopping to think about it and never looking for alternative solutions. This is probably because my parents were always fighting about money. In my mind money and confrontation are linked.'

'I hated thinking about money. The idea of sorting out my finances struck me as incredibly boring. For years nothing would induce me to spend any time understanding money or how to manage it.'

## Knowledge is power

The best way to develop a more positive approach to money is to gain a reasonable knowledge of how personal finance works. What I mean by this is that you should:

- Identify the things about your own behaviour with regard to money that may be costing you time, energy and, of course, hard cash.
- Understand what you want from money. Do you have financial goals? Are they feasible?
- Work out how far you have got towards reaching your financial goals.
- Learn about the different ways you can achieve your financial goals. Look at alternative strategies. Discover what financial products and other support may be there to help you.
- Where you need professional help, make an informed decision on who you are going to trust.

Sounds like a lot to do? Don't panic. It is easier than you may think. In fact, in my experience, *everything listed above can be achieved in a matter of hours*. What's more, all the information you require to take action is to be found in this book or on my web site — www.moneydoctor.ie.

There is nothing complicated about personal finance. Once you get into it you may find it much more fascinating than you previously imagined.

## The benefits of taking more interest in your own money

By getting to grips with your own finances you could end up transforming your life. For instance, you could:

- Wipe out all your personal debts;
- Pay off your mortgage years early;
- Never have to borrow again;
- Have enough money to afford things which are important to you. An education for your children, for instance. Or a second home;
- Have enough money to retire early;
- Know that you and your dependents are protected against financial hardship; and
- Be wealthy enough never to worry about the future — whatever it may bring.

## MONEY DOCTOR WEALTH CHECK

*How to earn €2,400 every year for just 24 hours' work*

Still not sure if it is worth your while to take a greater interest in your personal finances? Would it make a difference if you were paid about €2,400 every year to do it? Well, that's what it could easily be worth to you if you become your own accountant.

In my experience, this is how much time it takes the average person to manage their personal finances properly:

| | |
|---|---|
| Picking up the background information they need, such as reading this book a couple of times: | c. 10 hours |
| Taking stock of their financial position: | c. 2 hours |
| Formulating a financial plan: | c. 6 hours |

Rearranging their financial affairs: c. 6 hours

Total initial commitment: c. 24 hours

Now, let's look at the sort of benefits the average person can reap:

Saving on better mortgage deal
(size of mortgage €200,000): c. €2,000

Saving on personal loan, car loan,
credit cards and overdraft: c. €200

Saving on insurance — life, health,
critical illness, payment protection
and motor: c. €120

Extra gains on savings and pension: c. €120

All the assumptions I have made are based on someone with an average income and an average amount of debt. The key point is:

**If you spend 24 hours on your financial affairs over the coming year — that's just two hours a month — it could be worth as much as €2,440 to you in the first year, or even more. That equates to €100 an hour for the initial time spent and with a little tweaking every other year, the total savings over the 25 years of an average mortgage can amount to a staggering €46,000.**

## Slowly does it

If I have one piece of advice to offer anyone wishing to put their finances on a firmer footing: don't rush it! Resist the temptation to charge in and instigate a lot of changes. Resist the temptation to make a lot of resolutions about how you are going to manage your money in the future. Better, in my experience, to take it slowly and steadily. Set aside a few hours now to read this book. Then set aside a regular time to put what you learn into practice. A couple of hours a month may well be enough. Before you do anything at all, learn to think positively. Your ultimate goal must be to make a lifetime commitment to making your hard-earned money work for you.

## A positive outcome

What does it mean, in practice, to think positively about money? Here are the sorts of things people have said to me *after* they have changed their attitude to money:

'I found out that I am not useless at handling money, after all. It is much easier and more satisfying than I imagined.'

'I manage my money properly now. I no longer waste it and I no longer worry.'

'I am using what I have got to much better effect. You don't have to have a huge income to be rich.'

'I am enjoying my money for the first time.'

'Now I am honest about money. I understand it and as a result I have been able to take control.'

This last quote sums up the most important thing I have learned about developing a more positive approach to money: once you understand it, you'll find it much easier to control.

*The Money Doctor says ...*

- Before you start looking at your financial position in detail, spend a little time thinking through your relationship with money.

- It is important to develop a positive attitude to money. If you are afraid, confused or bored by money, you are hampering your chances of financial success.

- Don't view sorting out your finances as a one-off activity to be dealt with as quickly as possible. Learn to make looking after your money a part of your life.

- Need more motivation? In my experience, someone on an average income with average levels of debt and savings *can make themselves €46,000 better off over their working life* just by spending a few hours sorting out their finances. That's a lot of cash for not much effort.

# 2

## LEARN TO
## SPEAK THE LANGUAGE

### A QUICK GUIDE TO THE MOST
### IMPORTANT PERSONAL FINANCE
### TERMINOLOGY

One of the first things about finance that puts people off is the language. The moment an expert starts to bandy around terms like 'dividend', 'yield', 'compound interest' and 'net present value', it all starts to sound very intimidating.

Like every other area of life, finance has a specialised language. It has its own jargon. Jargon is actually very useful; we need precise terms that are clearly defined so that there is no confusion about what is being said. On the other hand if you don't understand what the jargon means, you are automatically at a disadvantage. Financial institutions are obliged to use legal phrasing and disclaimers to describe their products but, unfortunately, this can also confuse their customers. And customers who don't understand something are hardly in a position to ask awkward questions, or to compare value for money.

In this chapter we will, therefore, look at four important terms used in personal finance. Never again will you be dependent on someone else to explain any of the following to you:

- Percentages;
- The difference between capital and income;
- Compound interest; and

- Gearing.

*Other terminology you may find useful is explained in the 'Jargon Buster' section at the back of this book.*

## Percentages Made Easy

### *You are not alone*

If you aren't entirely comfortable with percentages you are not alone. People in most walks of life are not trained to work out the 'yield' on their investment property, or even how to calculate an interest-only repayment on their mortgage. Life is lived at such a fast pace nowadays that people just about have time to direct their attention on the two most important facets of their lives: family and work. Is it any wonder that the majority of people struggle to sort out their money matters?

### *What is a percentage?*

The word 'percentage' literally means 'parts per 100' — 'cent' being the Latin word for 100. Because percentages always deal with parts per 100 they allow you to compare things that would otherwise be very difficult to compare. They are particularly useful when it comes to choosing a loan or deciding on the relative worth of different investment opportunities.

For instance, 85% of home borrowers in the United States use a financial adviser rather than go direct to a lender. In the UK, 65% of borrowers use an adviser, while here in Ireland less than 40% of borrowers go to an independent adviser.

## *How to work out percentages*

You calculate the percentage by turning your numbers into a fraction, divide it out and then multiply by 100.

To give an example of how percentages are used as a basis of comparison I'm going to use an analogy from one of the other great passions of my life: football.

Imagine you are the manager of a Premiership team and you have three footballers who specialise in taking penalty kicks. You want to establish which of the three is the most effective or has the highest score rate. You could, of course, have all three take 20 penalties each against a top-class goalkeeper, with the player scoring the most being judged the best. However, the only real comparison should be based on their performance in the heat of battle over the course of a number of seasons. The figures could look as follows:

|                  | Player A | Player B | Player C |
|------------------|----------|----------|----------|
| Penalties taken: | 25       | 20       | 30       |
| Penalties scored:| 22       | 17       | 24       |

From the above figures it is obvious that in absolute terms Player C has scored the most goals, but which player is the most effective? If you express these figures in percentage terms the answer then becomes clear.

*Player A* converted 22 of his 25 penalties so the calculation would look as follows:

$$\frac{22}{25} \times 100 = 88\%.$$

If you were using a calculator you would key it in like this: $22 \div 25 \times 100$.

*Player B* converted 17 of his 20 penalties so the calculation would be as follows:

$$\frac{17}{20} \times 100 = 85\%.$$

*Player C* converted 24 of his 30 penalties so the calculation would be as follows:

$$\frac{17}{20} \times 100 = 80\%.$$

Converting numbers to percentages allows us to make a fair comparison between the penalty skills of the three players. Player C converted 80% of his penalties, Player B converted 85% of his penalties, but Player A, with an 88% success rate, is clearly the best.

## MONEY DOCTOR WEALTH WARNING

*Don't trust your calculator*

Don't always believe the answer the calculator gives you. Why not? Because the tiniest slip of your finger could give you a completely wrong answer without you being aware of it. Here are five things you can do to avoid calculator error:

1. Estimate your answer before you begin a calculation;

2. Do every calculation twice;

3. Know your calculator;

4. Don't be overawed by your calculator; and

5. Hang on to common sense and what you know.

# The Vital Difference between Capital and Income

## *All money is not equal*

One of the most important financial concepts to understand is the difference between capital and income. Capital is something — it could be money, a property, shares or some other investment — that generates an income for whomever owns it. A good way to remember the difference is to think of a fruit tree. The tree itself is the 'capital'. The fruit it produces is the 'income'. You continue to own the tree (capital) and it continues to bear fruit (income) every year. Your wage or salary is the income which comes from the capital of your labour, hence the expression 'human capital'. Money is not just money — it is either capital or income.

## *And then there is 'interest'*

When you own capital and it produces an income, you have a number of choices:

- You can hold on to the capital and spend the income;
- You can hold on to the capital, add the income to it, and generate even more income; or
- You can dispose of some or all of the capital and thus reduce the income you receive.

Let us go to the farmyard for an example and use chickens and eggs! You have some hens (capital) which lay eggs (income). You can do one of three things:

- You can hold on to the chickens (capital) and eat the eggs (income);
- You can hold on to the chickens (capital) and leave the eggs to hatch into more chickens (more capital) that in turn will produce even more eggs (income) for you; or

- You can eat your chickens (thus eating into your capital) and thus reduce the total amount of eggs (income) you receive.

There are lots of different names for the income produced by capital. In the case of property, for instance, it is called rental income. In the case of a cash deposit in a bank, it is called interest.

## The Miracle of Compound Interest

### *A financial concept that can make — or break — you*

When you are earning it, it has the power to make you very rich. When you are paying it, it has the power to make you very poor. Albert Einstein described it as 'the greatest mathematical discovery of all time'. It is the reason why banks, building societies, credit card companies and other financial institutions make so much profit from lending money. And it is the reason why ordinary investors can make themselves rich simply by doing nothing. It is a fiendishly simple concept called 'compound interest'.

### *Compound interest in one easy lesson*

Perhaps the easiest way to understand compound interest is to look at a hypothetical example. Imagine that you have €1,000 and that you invest it in a savings account which pays interest at a rate of 10% per year. At the end of one year you will be entitled to €100 interest. If you withdraw this interest but leave your capital, at the end of the second year you will be entitled to another €100 interest. Supposing, however, that you don't withdraw the interest but leave it to 'compound'. At the end of your first year your €1,000 is worth €1,100. At the end of your second year you will have earned €110 interest, meaning that your original €1,000 is worth €1,210. Put another way, your interest is earning you more interest.

> You will sometimes see the initials C.A.R. in relation to interest. This is the Compound Annual Rate … in other words, it is the amount of interest you will receive if you keep adding your interest to your capital in the way I have just described.

Now let's look at a real example. According to research, the Irish stock market has produced an annual average nominal return of 14% since 1989.

> **At this rate, if you invested €1,000 today it would be worth €3,700 in ten years' time.**

Still not impressed? How much do you think your money would grow by if, at the age of 25, you had started saving €100 a month (that's €25 a week) for just ten years at the same return? €15,000? €18,000? You are not close. At the age of 35 your money would be worth €25,000. Better still, if you continued saving at the same rate for a further 30 years, at the age of 65 your money would be worth €1.5m.

Obviously this is a very simple example and does not take into account any taxes, management charges etc., and the rates of return used here may never be available again. My main purpose is to show the effect of compound interest over the longer term.

## *No wonder lenders love you*

When you borrow money, compound interest is working

against you. Supposing, for instance, you borrow €5,000 on a credit card at an interest rate of 15% — which isn't high by today's standards. The credit card company allows you to make a minimum payment of 1.5% each month. After two years you will still owe approx €4,700, having made repayments of €1,750, of which €1,450 has been swallowed up in interest. Figure out for yourself, if you have the stamina to calculate the payments, how long it will take you to pay off the full debt.

Compound interest is your greatest enemy *and* your greatest ally. When you are in debt, it works against you. But when you have money to invest, you can make compound interest work for you.

## The Value of Gearing

### *Allowing other people to make you rich*

Using borrowed money to buy an asset is called gearing. If you can make it work in your favour, gearing can dramatically boost your profits. For instance:

> Supposing you buy a €200,000 apartment using a €40,000 deposit and a €160,000 mortgage. After one year the apartment is worth €240,000. It isn't just that you have made a €40,000 profit — you've actually doubled the €40,000 you originally invested. In other words, you've achieved a 100% gain in just 12 months.

Even if you deduct the mortgage interest you've had to pay for the year you've owned your apartment, you have still done very well. However, what goes up can also come down. In the UK, between 1987 and 1989, house prices *fell by around one third*. If this happened to someone selling an apartment they bought for €200,000 using a €160,000 mortgage, they would not only have seen their €40,000 deposit wiped out, they would owe an additional €26,666 (the difference between the mortgage of €160,000 and the €133,334 you would get for the apartment). When this happens, it is called being in 'negative equity'.

> Gearing is the easiest and most effective way of increasing the potential profit from any investment. It is also the most effective way of increasing the potential loss, something every investor contemplating gearing would be well advised to remember.

There is a commonly held view that owning property is a one-way bet. But in the recent history of many European countries there have been periods when residential property prices fell. In fact, over the long term, the Irish stock market has out-performed Irish property. Furthermore, it is vitally important to diversify your investments, thus spreading your risk.

Many people re-mortgage their homes in order to have a deposit with which to buy a second investment property. This can be a very sensible thing to do. However, if you have an existing mortgage on your home, it might make more sense to invest in another area — such as the stock market. But it very much depends on your circumstances.

Without gearing, most of us would never be able to own our own homes. It also allows us to make other highly lucrative investments. Nevertheless, you should think carefully before you embark on any investment that requires you to borrow money. You want to make sure that the investment is going to earn you more than the loan is going to cost you.

*The Money Doctor says ...*

- It is well worth your while to practice calculating percentages as these are the most common way of comparing both investment and lending products.

- If you are trying to remember the difference between capital and income think of an apple tree. The tree is your capital and its annual crop of fruit is your income.

- Compound interest can make you rich and it can make you poor too. In the case of an investment it is the process whereby the interest you earn from something is added to the capital to produce even more interest. In the case of a loan it is the process whereby the interest you owe is added to the capital, making it harder to get out of debt.

- Gearing allows you to buy an asset with borrowed money. There is no better way to achieve dramatic investment returns but, remember, it can work the other way too.

- You'll find a full explanation of all the most commonly used financial expressions and terms in the Jargon Buster section at the back of this book.

# 3

## A FIRST-CLASS PLAN

### HOW TO SOLVE ALL YOUR FINANCIAL WORRIES, SAVE YOURSELF TIME AND MAKE YOURSELF SUBSTANTIALLY RICHER

I am afraid that financial planning has got itself a bit of a bad name. This is unfair because a financial plan is only a way of getting you from where you are to where you want to be. If you dream of freeing yourself from debt, owning your own home, being able to retire in comfort, paying for your children's education, or anything else for that matter, then a financial or money plan makes sound sense. Put another way, if you adopt a haphazard approach to money you risk failing to meet your financial objectives. This short chapter explains why creating a money plan is so important. The next chapter looks at the subject in greater detail.

## What should go into a money plan

The key elements of a money plan should be:

- A description of what you want — your financial goals;
- A description of what you have already achieved in money terms; and
- The different actions you need to take to realise your ambitions.

In the next chapter we'll look at all of this in detail. For now all I really want is to persuade you of the importance of creating a plan. Perhaps it would help to think about it this way:

If you were driving from, say, Paris to Moscow you would not choose a road at random and hope that it would take you where you want to get. Rather, you would plan your journey in advance. If, as you travelled, you encountered diversions you would get out your map and decide on a new route. Throughout the journey you would check your progress.

Your money plan should have the same qualities. That is to say it should:

- Help you reach your destination;
- Make your journey as fast as possible;
- Stop you from wasting time or energy;
- Help you avoid frustration along the way;
- Be flexible enough to cope with anything that might otherwise delay you; and
- Make your journey enjoyable.

One more point. It is vital that your money plan takes into account all your financial desires — both while you are alive and after you are dead. A money plan that only covers a specific, short-term requirement (for instance, saving for your retirement) isn't going to bring you lasting financial success.

## Looking at the complete picture

It is human nature to compartmentalise money decisions. Let me give you just three examples:

- When you want to buy a home you look for a mortgage;
- When you begin to think about retirement you start a pension; and
- When you have a young family you take out life insurance.

It is also human nature to respond to *ad hoc* situations as they arise — for example, subscribing for newly-issued shares on a whim or paying for education fees when you hadn't expected to do so.

The trouble with this haphazard approach is that it is both wasteful and risky because:

- You may end up spending more than you have on borrowing money;
- You may waste money unnecessarily on tax;
- You may end up with inferior and expensive financial products;
- You may risk your capital, your income and the standard of living of you and your dependents;
- You may miss opportunities; and
- You may make yourself unhappy worrying about your financial security.

Personal financial planning should be holistic, in other words, it should take into account your complete situation. It should also minimise your risk and provide you with the structure to achieve your financial aims. Crucially, it should concentrate not on 'finance' but on you and what you want. What are your dreams? What are your ambitions? Where do you want to go to in life?

## MONEY DOCTOR WEALTH CHECK

*Yes, creating a money plan will be good for your financial health*
Please put aside any misgivings you might have about creating your own money plan ...

- You don't have to be fabulously wealthy.

- It won't involve a great deal of time or effort.

- It is anything but boring.

- You won't have to fraternise with high-pressure salesmen.

- It won't mark you out as someone who takes their finances too seriously.

## MONEY DOCTOR WEALTH CHECK

*Where there's a will ... there's a relative*

Do you have a will? If you have, when did you last update it? Are you taking *full* advantage of all the tax allowances and exemptions to make sure that your beneficiaries don't have to pay unnecessary inheritance tax?

If you are over eighteen (or if you are younger, but married) you should draw up a will. If you don't, your money will be distributed in accordance with the Succession Act of 1965. This means that your estate could end up not going to your chosen beneficiary or beneficiaries but filling instead the government's coffers.

You'll find more information about using your will to save tax on the Money Doctor web site www.moneydoctor.ie. Don't forget, both you and your partner should draw up a will and you should also consider:

- Giving a power of attorney to someone you trust should you become physically incapacitated.

> • A living will explaining anything you would like
> done should you become so unwell as to be
> unable to communicate.

## What your money plan should look like

Your money plan may be no more than a single piece of
paper on which you have jotted a few appropriate notes.
You might think of it in the same way that you think of a
career plan or any other life plan. It is there to guide you,
to save you time, and to ensure that none of your effort is
wasted.

## Help is at hand

In the next chapter we will look at each individual element of
a money plan, along with real-life examples, and in a later
chapter we will consider how to choose an adviser.

Whether or not you ask a professional financial planner to
help you write your money plan and/or organise your
finances, I believe it is vital that you have a good
understanding of all the issues at stake. Make the decision to
create your own money plan and you are more than half way
there.

> *The Money Doctor says ...*
> • Financial planning is about getting you from
> where you are, in money terms, to where you
> want to be, as quickly and as effortlessly as
> possible.

- Create your own money plan so that you are able to fulfil all your financial ambitions. Don't trust to luck.

- Your money plan will ensure that you make the most of your money.

- Take the decision to invest a few hours in creating your money plan — all you need to do is read the next chapter!

# 4

## HOW TO WRITE A MONEY PLAN

### THE ONLY WAY TO GUARANTEE YOUR FINANCIAL DREAMS COME TRUE

Writing a personal financial or money plan is simplicity itself and in this chapter you will find all the guidance you need.

## Start by dreaming

The first thing to do is to *stop* thinking about money for a few minutes. Instead, put your mind to what you really want. Dream a little and while you dream try and come up with answers to the following questions:

- What would you like to be doing in, say, five years time? Ten years? Fifteen years? Twenty years?
- What work, if any, will you be doing?
- Where do you see yourself living?
- How do you imagine spending your leisure time?
- What is your family situation?

Financial planning has one objective: to make your dreams come true. It does this by taking all the different things you want and then identifying all the different things you need to do to make them happen. Here are just three case histories of people I know who have gone through this process:

- Pamela, a teacher, was determined to pay off all her debts (including her mortgage) so that she could retire at age fifty and concentrate on her hobbies. She wrote a money plan and took the appropriate action and is now just two years away from achieving her goal.

- Ian, a bus driver, only began to think about a pension on his forty-seventh birthday. With a relatively young family to support, cash was tight. However, with the help of a money plan and a bit of financial reorganisation Ian can now look forward to a much more comfortable retirement.
- Joe, a structural engineer, wanted to make a career change but felt he couldn't afford to without any savings in place. With the help of a money plan he re-prioritised certain aspects of his life and is now well on the way to building a very substantial amount of capital.

In each case they decided what they wanted first — more leisure time, a pension, a career change — and then worked out what they had to do to achieve it. You should go through the same process:

- What has to happen for you to realise your ambitions?
- When does it have to happen?
- What income will you need?
- What capital will you need?
- How is it going to happen?

## Different phases of life bring different needs

When trying to sort out your financial objectives it may help to divide your life into different phases. Here are a few pointers.

### *Young and free*

When you are young you tend not to think too far into the future. Your financial priorities should include:

- Creating an emergency fund to cover unexpected expenses;
- Paying off any personal or student loans;
- Short-term saving for cars, holidays and so forth;
- Income protection in case you are unable to work for any reason;
- Starting a pension plan (it is never too early!); and
- Saving for major purchases, such as the deposit to buy a home.

## Family life

If you settle down with a partner your financial priorities will almost certainly alter — especially if you have children. Now you will be thinking about:

- Creating an emergency fund;
- Protecting both your incomes (if relevant) in case you are unable to work;
- Life assurance for both you and your partner;
- Buying a home with the help of a mortgage;
- Planning for education fees (if you have children), whether for private school or university;
- Retirement planning; and
- Short-term saving for cars, holidays and so forth.

By the time many people settle down they have already built up sizeable debts. Where this is the case, becoming debt-free must be a priority (advice on how to do this quickly and painlessly is to be found in Chapter 8).

## The middle years

Financial priorities in your middle years will vary according to how much money you have earned during your twenties and thirties, and how you have spent or invested it. For some it can be a period of relative affluence with a higher level of disposable income becoming available. For others it is a period of worry as retirement looms. Your priorities may include any or all of the following:

- Creating an emergency fund;
- Protecting both your incomes (if relevant) in case you are unable to work;
- Life assurance for both you and your partner;
- Paying off your mortgage and any other debts;
- Retirement planning;
- Short-term saving for cars, holidays and so forth;
- Long-term care planning if you are worried that your pension and/or the State may not provide for you sufficiently.

Although pension planning should have been a priority as soon as you started work, the truth is that it is not until they are in their forties or even their fifties that many people begin to consider their retirement. Providing for a comfortable old age may, therefore, be the most pressing need.

## *In retirement*

With luck your retirement will be comfortable. Your debts should all be paid. You should have a range of assets, not least your own home and a pension fund. You should have spare cash to indulge your chosen leisure activities. Now your priorities are likely to include any or all of the following:

- Creating an emergency fund;
- Funding any benefits lost due to retirement, such as health insurance or a company car;
- Long-term care planning;

- Tax planning; and
- Investing for income or finding other ways to boost income.

## MONEY DOCTOR WEALTH CHECK

*Things to consider when setting financial objectives*

*Protecting your family*
If you died suddenly do you have dependants who would still need an income? How much? Would they also need capital (to repay a mortgage, for instance)? How much? Do you need to take out life assurance? Is your existing cover adequate? Are you paying too much for it?

*Protecting your income*
If you were unable to work due to an illness or accident would your employer continue to pay you? For how long? Would it be enough money to meet your obligations? Do you have savings to fall back on? Do you need to take out permanent health insurance? Is your existing cover adequate? Are you paying too much for it?

*Note: Permanent health insurance is known as PHI. This is very different to VHI which is a form of medical insurance. See the* Jargon Buster *at the back of the book for a detailed explanation.*

### Buying your own home

Do you need to save up money to use as a deposit to buy your own home? How much will you need? How long will it take you? If you have a home could you save money by switching mortgage? Would you like to pay your mortgage off early? What type of mortgage best suits your needs?

### Becoming debt-free

Do you owe money because of credit cards, store cards, personal loans, car loans, secured loans, hire purchase agreements or any other sort of debt? How much? How long will it take you to pay it off on your current repayment plan? Should you reorganise your finances to pay off the debt faster and to save money?

### Care in old age

Will you be happy relying on the State? Should you make other provisions, either through insurance or by saving extra money?

### Medical care

Are you happy to rely on the State? Should you take out private medical insurance?

### Your saving and investment targets

Do you have an emergency fund to cover unexpected expenses? Do you save for major

> purchases such as cars or home renovations? What are your investment targets? Are you investing in order to have a lump sum or for income? How much can you afford to invest? If you have a pension in place will it be sufficient for your needs? Should you be changing your investment strategy?

## Setting realistic aims

If you had unlimited funds then you could achieve all your financial ambitions without difficulty and you wouldn't need a money plan. As it is, for most of us life is more complicated. Since we can't have everything we want instantly, we need to set realistic targets and work towards them in easy stages. To make sure we have realistic targets we must test them. Let me give you an example:

David is 40 and self-employed. His objective is to be financially independent by the age of 55. At that point he wants to be able to live comfortably without working. His current income is €40,000 a year and he feels that he will be able to manage on much less, say €25,000 a year, once he retires. To achieve this he will need capital resources of between €500,000 and €600,000. At this point in time he has a pension worth €100,000 which, if it grows in real terms (i.e. after the effects of inflation) by 5% a year, will be worth some €208,000 in fifteen years. He also has €25,000 of stocks and shares which he expects to grow at a slightly faster rate, say 7.5% a year, which would mean an extra €74,000 in fifteen years.

In other words, David has a shortfall of between €212,000 and €312,000. To fill this shortfall he should save at least €600 a month (assuming a growth rate of at least 7.5%) until he reaches 55. €600 a month, or more, is a lot of cash to find, so David may have to adjust his expectations. Perhaps he could live on less? Or postpone his retirement an extra five years?

Once you have settled on your overall objectives you will have to decide which is the most important to you. Would you rather pay off your mortgage ten years early or take an annual holiday overseas? Is being able to retire early more important than putting your children through private school?

There are other priorities to weigh up. I always recommend that those with or without dependants take out income protection insurance before they take out life cover. Why? Anyone under retirement age is twenty times more likely to be unable to work for a prolonged period due to sickness than they are to die. Another recommendation I often make is that people with high personal debt pay it off or consolidate it before they start saving money. This is because it costs more to borrow than you can hope to earn from most forms of low-risk investment.

Anyway, the two key points I want to make are:

- Keep your financial expectations realistic; and
- Test them to make sure.

## How far have you got?

If the first stage of a money plan involves deciding what you want, and what you need to achieve it, then the second stage is all about working out where you have got to so far. You need to produce an honest and realistic assessment of:

- What resources you have;
- What demands there are on your resources; and
- What you are already doing to meet your targets.

Once you have this information you will know what surplus is available to you and whether you have a shortfall that needs to be made up.

If you visit my web site — *www.moneydoctor.ie* — you'll find several aids to help you make and reach your goals. Otherwise, you can use the questionnaire that follows.

### Your monthly income and outgoings

I usually suggest that people start with their income and, if relevant, their spouse/partner's income. The best way to calculate this is as follows:

| Monthly income — gross | You € | Spouse/Partner € |
|---|---|---|
| Salary or wages: | _____ | _____ |
| Profits from business: | _____ | _____ |
| Investment income: | _____ | _____ |
| State benefits: | _____ | _____ |
| Pensions: | _____ | _____ |
| Other earnings: | _____ | _____ |
| Anything else: | _____ | _____ |
| **Subtotal A:** | €_____ | |
| Less tax (PRSI & income tax): | _____ | _____ |
| **Subtotal B:** | €_____ | |

The resulting figure (Subtotal B) is your disposable income. You now need to consider how you spend it.

| Monthly outgoings | You € | Spouse/Partner € |
|---|---|---|
| Rent/mortgage: | | |
| Utilities (gas, electricity, telephone, etc.): | | |
| Food: | | |
| Household items: | | |
| Drink: | | |
| Car(s): | | |
| Home insurance: | | |
| Life insurance: | | |
| Other insurance: | | |
| Clothes: | | |
| Child-related expenses: | | |
| Credit cards: | | |
| Other loan repayments: | | |
| Spending money: | | |
| Pension contribution: | | |
| Regular saving plans: | | |
| Anything else: | | |
| **Subtotal C:** | € | |

By subtracting your monthly outgoings (Subtotal C) from your disposable income (Subtotal B) you will arrive at your available surplus. Don't despair if this is a 'minus' figure. That's why you are reading this book and, together, we are going to do something about it!

## Your Assets

Working out what assets you have involves the same process as working out what your surplus income is. You need to tot up the value of everything you own and subtract any debts or other liabilities you may have.

Start with a list of the assets themselves:

| Assets | You € | Spouse/Partner € |
|---|---|---|
| Home: | _____ | _____ |
| Personal belongings: | _____ | _____ |
| Furniture and contents of home: | _____ | _____ |
| Car(s): | _____ | _____ |
| Other property: | _____ | _____ |
| Other valuables: | _____ | _____ |
| Cash: | _____ | _____ |
| Savings: | _____ | _____ |
| Shares: | _____ | _____ |
| Other investments: | _____ | _____ |
| **Subtotal D:** | €_____ | |

With regard to any investments you have, such as savings plans or a pension, you may want to work out what they will be worth at whatever point in the future you intend to cash them in. This can be a complex business. A pension fund, for instance, may grow by more or less than the predicted amount. Therefore, it could be well worth your while to get professional assistance with your calculations.

## Your Liabilities

| Liabilities | You € | Spouse/Partner € |
|---|---|---|
| Mortgage: | _____ | _____ |
| Credit card debts: | _____ | _____ |
| Personal loans: | _____ | _____ |
| Hire purchase: | _____ | _____ |
| Overdraft: | _____ | _____ |
| Other loans: | _____ | _____ |
| Tax: | _____ | _____ |
| Other liabilities: | _____ | _____ |
| **Subtotal E:** | €_____ | |

By subtracting your total liabilities (Subtotal E) from the value of your assets (Subtotal D) you will arrive at what financial experts call your 'net worth'. While it is not good if this is a 'minus' figure, you shouldn't despair. The whole purpose of a money plan is to strengthen your finances.

## Making assumptions

All financial planning requires assumptions to be made. Some of these assumptions will be personal to you, such as how much income you will earn in the future. Other assumptions will be related to factors only partly within your control, such as the return you can expect to receive from a particular investment. You will also need to allow for financial factors beyond your control, such as the state of the economy.

> When making assumptions, the longer the period you are planning for, the less accurate your assumptions will be. It is very hard to predict exactly what you will be earning in, say, five or ten years, let alone what you will be earning in twenty years.

In order to improve the quality of their assumptions many people use historic figures for guidance. Below are some statistics that you may find of help. An explanation of all the technical terms is to be found in the Jargon Buster at the back of this book.

## Inflation

There was a time when inflation had the single greatest influence on the economy and thus on financial planning. Although inflation has been quite low for the last few years it still has a marked affect on the cost of borrowing *and* the value of your investments.

The best way to think of inflation is in terms of how much actual money you will need in the future to enjoy the same spending power as you enjoy today. Even low levels of inflation make a big difference as the chart below shows:

*What you will need to pay for what €1 buys today if the annual rate of inflation averages …*

|                | 2%     | 3%     | 4%     | 5%     |
|----------------|--------|--------|--------|--------|
| After 5 years  | €1.10  | €1.16  | €1.22  | €1.28  |
| After 10 years | €1.22  | €1.34  | €1.81  | €2.08  |
| After 20 years | €1.49  | €1.81  | €2.67  | €3.40  |

Clearly, even a 2% rate of inflation erodes the real value of your money over quite short periods of time. For this reason I always recommend deducting the expected average rate of inflation from the expected average return of savings and investments. For example, assume that you can earn 6.5% return on your investments and inflation is 2.5%. That means that your real return, in terms of actual spending power, is just 4%. In cash terms that means each €100 invested will bring you €4 a year income *not* allowing for any tax. In terms of borrowing you must also remember that if inflation pushes up interest rates, a larger percentage of your income may go on servicing your debts, another reason to pay them off sooner rather than later! Finally, bear in mind that the projections you get from unit trusts, pension providers and so forth don't make any allowance for inflation.

Here are the inflation figures in Ireland for the last 20 years:

Over the last 10 years inflation has averaged 3.20% a year.

Over the last 20 years inflation has averaged 3.50% a year.

## Interest rates

Interest rates vary dramatically depending on whether you are borrowing or investing. In the case of borrowing there is an even larger difference between the different types of loan. For instance, in 2002, when a typical mortgage cost 5% per annum, you could pay up to 20% on a typical store card.

## Mortgage rates

Over the last ten years the average mortgage rate has been 7% a year.

## Personal loan rates

Over the last ten years the average personal loan rate has been 12% a year.

## Bank or building society deposit rates

Over the last ten years the average rate for deposits has been 3% a year.

## Investments

Not only do the returns on different types of investment vary dramatically, so do the returns within each sort of investment vehicle. So, while investing in the stock market brings a much better average return than investing in property, an individual investor might do substantially better or worse. In general, it is best to spread your money between different types of investment and to assume an average return of between 4% and 7% in real terms.

## Return from government bonds

Over the last ten years the average return has been 4.7% a year.

## *Return from the stock market*

Over the last 10 years the average return has been 10.1% a year.

## Working out how much capital you will need ...

One of the hardest calculations anyone has to make is how much capital they should have to provide a sufficient income for their needs. There are different factors affecting this: inflation, tax and investment performance.

On the whole, my advice is to assume a 2.5% return after inflation and tax. Using this assumption you will see below how much capital you need to produce different levels of income.

| *Amount of annual income* € | *Amount of capital required* € |
|---|---|
| 1,000 | 40,000 |
| 5,000 | 200,000 |
| 10,000 | 400,000 |
| 15,000 | 600,000 |
| 20,000 | 800,000 |
| 25,000 | 1,000,000 |
| 30,000 | 1,200,000 |
| 35,000 | 1,400,000 |
| 40,000 | 1,600,000 |
| 45,000 | 1,800,000 |
| 50,000 | 2,000,000 |

## The personal factor

You are almost ready to commit your money plan to paper. So far you have:

- Identified and prioritised your money objectives;
- Examined what resources you have available;
- Taken into account any shortfalls;
- Revised your targets in light of available resources; and
- Made assumptions regarding external factors such as inflation.

But there is still one other thing you need to consider: the personal factor. That is to say, the other influences which are going to have a major effect on your ability to meet your money targets. These will include:

- Your personality. There is no point in coming up with a really good money plan if you don't tailor it to suit your personality. If you think you may have trouble sticking to the plan, you need either to change the plan or try and change your approach (as explained in Chapter 1).
- Tax. It is essential that you consider the impact of tax on your financial planning, especially when looking at your savings and investments. In Chapter 16 you'll find useful advice to minimise the effect of tax on your plan.
- Your attitude to risk. Are you someone who gives a high priority to security? Or are you perfectly content with a high degree of risk? How much risk you feel comfortable with will, naturally, influence your financial planning.
- Your timing. Some financial aims are short-term, some long-term, and some open-ended. Your age is a major factor in determining many money goals. By the same token you need to bear in mind that many financial

products are designed for specific periods of time and may be wholly inappropriate for some of your money targets.

- Your health. This will influence the sort of insurance you should (and can) take out, as well as which investment products you should choose.

At this point you are probably starting to feel that I was joking when I said writing a money plan was simplicity itself. Once you look at the real-life examples below, however, you'll see that I was being perfectly serious. Your money plan does not have to be complex.

## Real-life examples

I already mentioned three real-life examples. Here are their individual money plans for you to consider.

### *Pamela*

Pamela is a teacher. When she first came to see the Money Doctor she was 36 and single. She has since married.

During her late twenties and early thirties Pamela got into the habit of borrowing money to pay for short-term spending such as holidays and clothes. So, although she owned her own home, she also had quite substantial debts.

Her money plan has only been designed to take her to the age of 50. When she reaches that point she intends to rethink her strategy, possibly working full- or part-time as a teacher for another five years in order to build up some extra savings.

You will notice that she has made paying off her debts a priority. She has also taken action to cut short the term of her mortgage. By doing this she is saving herself nine years of mortgage interest, that's a staggering €5,200.

Age: 36

*Money Ambition:* To be free of debt.

*Money Target:* €12,000 of accumulated debts from credit cards and personal loans to be paid off.

*Methodology:* Consolidate loans into her mortgage (see Chapter 8 for details) thus saving on interest rates and freeing up an additional €300 per month to pay mortgage off. Cut up credit cards and don't take out any more personal loans.

*Money Ambition:* To pay off mortgage by the age of 50.

*Money Target:* 23 years left of mortgage. Total amount borrowed €80,000

*Methodology:* Remortgage with current account mortgage. €92,000 total loan. Using the extra €300 per month now available, it will be possible to pay this off within 14 years.

*Money Ambition:* To build up an emergency fund of money.

*Money Target:* Cash for emergencies and also to cover things such as buying a car and paying for holidays.

*Methodology:* Save €200 a month. Whenever this fund reaches €3,000, use excess to pay off more of current account mortgage.

## *Ian*

Ian is a bus driver on an annual salary of €38,000. He consulted the Money Doctor when he turned 47 because he was worried about his pension arrangements. Having moved from job to job during his career he hadn't built up anything like enough money in his pension fund, a defined contribution fund worth about €50,000, to guarantee him a comfortable retirement. Furthermore, there is no guarantee that Ian will still be in the same occupation when he turns 65. Another problem Ian had was that two of his children had not yet left home, so not only was he still supporting them but there was always the possibility of third-level education to pay for. However, he has a virtually mortgage-free home valued at €400,000 and no other debts.

Also on the plus side, his wife has plans to go back to full-time employment, which would dramatically increase the family income. She estimates that she will earn in excess of €30,000 per annum.

Age: 47

---

*Money Ambition:* To ensure pension fund is sufficient to guarantee comfortable retirement.

*Money Target:* Pension shortfall estimated to be some €360,000.

*Methodology:* At 47, Ian can invest 25% of his annual income into a pension scheme — €791.66 per month and after tax relief at 42%, a net outlay of €459.41 per month. Even at that he will need to boost his pension fund with a lump sum investment if he wants to make any impact on the pension shortfall that will arise at age 65. Perhaps an equity release from the home should be considered for that lump sum investment — possibly €100,000 — especially since he now has the ability to repay for the next 20 years.

In addition to the above, equity could be released (at the same time as below) to fund the purchase of a buy-to-let property. This is also taking advantage of the ongoing property boom where the tenant is effectively funding your investment.

*Money Ambition:* To build up an emergency fund of money.

*Money Target:* Target is to have €10,000 saved to pay for emergencies and/or to help meet costs of third-level education.

*Methodology:* This equates to about three months net income for the rainy-day fund emergencies. From Ian's salary it would be impossible to save in the short term, so an equity release from the home to fund this and the possible third-level education needs would be a sensible approach, especially where his wife may now be able to make a financial contribution to the new mortgage.

*Money Ambition:* To protect income in case of illness, accident or redundancy.

*Money Target:* Ensure that the family wouldn't be hit financially for at least a year in the event of a crisis.

*Methodology:* Three products could be considered — **Serious Illness Cover,** where a lump sum is payable on contracting a serious illness. **Permanent Health Insurance,** which pays a regular monthly income — 66% of normal salary — until you retire or return to work, whichever is the sooner. **Repayment Protector insurance,** which pays your mortgage/loan for up to one year if you are sick, have an accident or are made redundant.

## *Joe*

Joe is a structural engineer. At 41 he is fed up with working for other people and wants to start up on his own. He feels that before he does this he should have a bit of extra cash behind him, just in case things don't work out. At the same time he wants to make sure that his pension doesn't suffer. Plus, he is conscious of the need to have extra insurance once he is freelance, just in case something happens.

Married with no children, his current income is €80,000 p.a. plus the usual bonuses and benefits. His wife, a hospital Sister, earns €52,000, while their home, valued at €650,000, has a mortgage of €150,000, attracting a 4.75% five-year fixed-rate maturing in four years time. They also have an unencumbered holiday home worth €180,000 and a residential investment property worth €350,000 with a €100,000 mortgage at a variable rate of 3.8%. Unfortunately, they have no great savings but did open two SSIAs which will be worth about €45,000 in mid-2006.

Age: 41

---

*Money Ambition:* Immediate cash to set up business and have a 'money cushion' for the first six months of operation

*Money Target:* €200,000 for the new business

*Methodology:* With no liquid resources, the obvious solution is equity release from his home, holiday home and/or residential investment property. It may well be worthwhile revisiting the home loan rate — it might benefit him to pay the fixed-rate penalty in order to avail of the lower tracker rates now available. Interest-only loans should also be considered as he could elect to pay €500 per month for that €200,000 for the next 30 years! Remember there are no penalties for lump sum payments on variable rate home loan mortgages.

---

*Money Ambition:* To be secure should he be unable to work or make his repayments. He also wishes to ensure his pension does not suffer.

*Money Target:* Life Cover of €300,000 and Serious Illness Cover €100,000, Permanent Health Insurance (or Income Protection) €5,000 per month

*Methodology:* Consider a complete revamp on all insurance — life and health cover. A complete appraisal of his pension may include leaving what he has in his fund but postponing future contributions to the fund until his business has taken off. He could also reinvest the two SSIAs on maturity in the fund in lieu of those non-payments as a single premium investment.

---

*Money Ambition:* Leverage the residential investment property to acquire another.

*Money Target:* Property to be acquired will cost €400,000 — needs all costs to be funded.

*Methodology:* Borrow €540,000 (against the two RIPs valued at €750,000 — loan to value of 72%) at 3.55% on an interest-only basis for the first ten years costing €1,597.50 per month. The borrowings include stamp duty of €30,000 plus €10,000 for legal fees and the entire purchase price of the new acquisition. Rental income for the two properties should well exceed repayments and take care of any tax liability on the rental income, together with a surplus.

---

### The Money Doctor says ...
- Whether or not you write up a formal money plan you'll gain a great deal simply from following the first few steps of the process.
- Work out your financial objectives. Decide what is most important to you. Think about what you will need to do to make your dreams come true.

- Assess how far you have got towards your target. Check that your target is realistic.
- Your money plan may have gaps in it and it may change over time, but it is an invaluable start to reorganising your finances and ensuring your long-term prosperity.

# 5

## MONEY IS A FAMILY AFFAIR

### HOW FAMILIES CAN WORK TOGETHER TO ACHIEVE LONG-TERM FINANCIAL SECURITY

Anyone who has been in a settled relationship will know that money and love can be a potent combination — both good and bad.

If you and your partner share the same attitude to money then obviously you'll be able to build a secure future for yourselves faster, more efficiently and more enjoyably than if you are in conflict. However, it would be ridiculous not to acknowledge that many relationships are blighted by arguments about money and that reaching a compromise is not always easy.

In this chapter we look at how couples, and families, can work together to reach their financial goals. And we also look at the importance of educating children about money.

## Problem? What problem?

All relationship/money problems tend to boil down to one or more of the following issues:

- How the money is earned and who is earning it;
- How the money is spent and who is spending it;
- How the money is being managed and who is managing it;

- How the money is being saved (if it is being saved at all) and who is doing the saving;
- How the money is being invested (if it is being invested at all) and who is handling the investment decisions; and
- What debts you have, both individually and jointly, and why they were incurred.

Of all the subjects which couples argue about, from the choice of holiday destination to who should do the washing-up, money arguments are the hardest to resolve. This is because our money beliefs tend to be a) firmly held, b) unconscious and c) non-negotiable.

Couples who are serious about building a financially secure future for themselves need to keep an open mind regarding their partner's viewpoint. One of you may be a saver, the other a spender, but that doesn't mean a compromise isn't possible.

**MONEY DOCTOR WEALTH CHECK**

*Are you and your partner financially compatible?*
When a couple disagree about money it is almost always because they each hold different money beliefs. Which of the following categories best describes you and your partner:

*Worry warts*
People who worry so much that they never really enjoy money — even when they have plenty.

*Big spenders*
People who spend money whether or not they have it. They don't mind going into debt to fund their lifestyle.

*Careful savers*
People who are committed to saving. Sometimes, however, they can be obsessive about it to the point of miserliness.

*Optimistic dreamers*
People who believe that through some miracle, perhaps an unexpected legacy or a lottery win, all their financial worries will be solved overnight.

*Outright fools*
People whose spending and borrowing is reckless.

*Clever planners*
People who plan for a secure financial future but still manage to enjoy a good lifestyle now.

Where a couple consists of two 'clever planners' you tend to get minimum friction. Otherwise, sooner or later, disagreements are bound to arise.

## In an ideal world

In an ideal world one would discuss money with a future partner before making any sort of commitment as this would allow you to check that you are financially compatible. However, we don't live in an ideal world and so most couples will find themselves tackling financial issues after they have been together for some time. Looking on the bright side, maybe this is preferable. After all, you now know and understand each other more.

## Opening a dialogue

The first and most important step for anyone in a relationship is to open a financial dialogue with their partner. If you don't communicate you won't know what they are thinking, and they won't know what you are thinking. My advice is to have a gentle discussion in which you raise some or all of the following topics:

- Your individual values in relation to money. What do each of you think is important?
- Any assumptions either of you may have. One of you may assume that finances should always be joint, the other may have fixed ideas about keeping them separate.
- Your dreams and desires and your partner's dreams and desires. How do you both envisage the future?
- Your fears and your partner's fears. What are you both most worried about?

Both of you will have inherited traits and you need to recognise what they are before any sort of agreement can be reached between you.

## Anything to declare?

There are so many tricky areas when it comes to discussing personal finance with your partner that it is hard to decide which is potentially the most controversial. One subject which never fails to cause problems is that of 'secret debts' and 'secret savings'. By this I mean:

- One or both partners have borrowed money without telling the other one.
- One or both partners have tucked money away without telling the other one.

Other 'secrets' which couples keep from each other include:

- How much one or other really earns.
- Money that one or the other has given away or promised (this often arises where one or other has been married before).

If you are harbouring a money secret from your partner, my advice would be to come clean. The longer you leave it, the worse it will be if you are discovered. Also, it is much harder (and sometimes impossible) to tackle your joint financial position if one of you is holding out.

**MONEY DOCTOR WEALTH CHECK**

*The gentle art of confession*
You have a money secret that you need to tell your partner. How can you do it without risking a break-up? Here are some tips:

- The longer you leave it, the worse it will be and the more chance that it will cause a serious rift.
- Pick your moment. No one likes to receive bad news just when they have to go to work or do something else. Better to raise the topic when you are alone and there is a chance to talk about it.

- If appropriate, don't forget to say 'sorry'.

A medical doctor once told me that he always prepares family members for news about the death of a loved one a day or two before it is likely to happen with the words: 'I am afraid you should expect the worst'. This gives them time to get used to the idea. If you start by saying you have a confession to make and that it may shock or anger them then the conversation is unlikely to be as acrimonious.

Don't fool yourself that, say, borrowing or spending money without telling your partner won't upset them. But, equally, remember that it is only money. The important thing is that there should be honesty in your relationship.

## Building a joint approach to money

Disagreements about personal finance can be very divisive. I have seen figures that suggest half of the couples who break up do so because of a disagreement about money. So when I say that you need to agree a joint financial strategy with your partner I don't say it lightly. One approach I have found works well is to:

- Look for common ground. It is likely, for instance, that you both want the same thing: to be free of debt and have plenty of spare cash;
- Communicate freely and honestly. Assess where you are and how each of you has contributed to the current state of affairs. Be honest. Discuss each of your strengths and weaknesses — the things you are doing right, and the things you are doing wrong; and

- Compromise. Don't allow past behaviour and events to poison your chance of success. Put grievances behind you. Start afresh and in doing so accept that you will both have to agree to do things differently in the future.

## Share out the chores

There are certain basic money chores that have to be done and one of the most useful things any couple can do in relation to their personal finances is to agree who is going to take on which responsibilities. My recommendation is that all major decisions are made jointly and that each partner should keep the other informed about what they are doing. The tasks that need to be divided up include:

- The paying of household bills;
- Filing and organising financial paperwork;
- Doing the household shopping;
- Checking the bank accounts and reconciling the balances;
- Looking after the spending money and accessing cash;
- Shopping for larger purchases;
- Saving money and arranging any loans;
- Investment decisions;
- Keeping an eye on investments; and
- Dealing with financial institutions, banks, insurance companies and so forth.

In many relationships one or other partner will take over management of the financial affairs. Even where this works without a hitch, I feel it is not entirely a good idea. Supposing one of you should die unexpectedly, how would the other cope? Also, what happens if you go your separate ways at some point? I can't stress how important it is to share information and decisions.

## MONEY DOCTOR WEALTH CHECK

*How to make yourself financially compatible*

Here are some valuable tips on handling joint finances, whether with your partner or with someone else, such as a flatmate or friend.

- Maintain your independence. A joint account is perfect for joint responsibilities but it is a good idea to keep an account for yourself so that you have money available to spend as you want. Decide which areas are joint expenditure and which you are each going to handle alone.

- If one half of a partnership takes over all the money management it can lead to big trouble. The person 'in charge' may end up resenting the fact that he or she is doing all the work, and he or she may also become controlling. The person not involved is leaving himself or herself vulnerable and is adopting an essentially childlike position. Both of you should take decisions together, even if one of you does the day-to-day accounting.

- Be honest about how you each feel. If one of you wants to save and the other wants to spend, admit it and work out a strategy that allows each of you to do as you please. Compromise!

- Plan for a future that isn't completely dependent on staying together. I realise that this may seem pessimistic but I frequently find myself counselling people who unexpectedly find themselves having to deal with money for the first time.

## The importance of involving and educating your children

Think about how your parents' approach to money influenced you. Now consider how your attitude will influence your own children. Regardless of your level of wealth, everything you say or do in relation to money will have an effect:

- If you don't discuss money in front of them they won't learn anything about it;
- Whatever emotions you display, such as fear, worry or indifference, will colour their own relationship with money; and
- If you are mean with money or overly generous, if you never waste a penny or if you spend like there's no tomorrow, your children will be watching and learning.

Given that they are unlikely to learn much about money from any other quarter, and given the way debt is spreading through society like some super-virus, it is obviously important that you educate your children about personal finance. You need to teach them the key principles, including how to:

- Save for a specific purpose;

- Stick to a budget;

- Choose competitive products;

- Shop around; and

- Spend money wisely.

> *The Money Doctor says …*
> My upbringing was fairly typical for Ireland in the 1960s. There were six of us squeezed into a three-bedroom house. My father was a quality control inspector and although we never went without, money was always tight. As a matter of course, we all took summer employment to help with the family finances and while it was tough at times, there was the satisfaction of knowing that we were earning money for the whole family. Today, I do sometimes wish that we didn't have quite so much so that our children could experience what it was like to have to work to put food on the table.

Clearly, what you don't want to do is worry your children about money. Still, I believe there is a lot to be said for showing them where your income comes from, and what you then do with it.

When your children realise how well you manage money, they can't fail to be proud of you. Naturally, they will grow up not just wanting to be debt-free and rich enough to retire when young, but actually understanding how this can be achieved. What better legacy could you leave?

> *The Money Doctor says …*
> • If you are in a relationship it is vital that you discuss your financial objectives together, sort out your differences and formulate a joint plan.

- Honesty is vital! You have to work together, not against each other.

- Remember, two heads are better than one. If you are working together you'll reach your objectives sooner, and it will be more fun, too.

- Don't forget, it is important to educate your children about finance. Don't let them leave home without good money habits and a genuine understanding of how money works.

# 6

## FINANCIAL PRODUCTS MADE EASY

### A QUICK INTRODUCTION TO ALL THE FINANCIAL PRODUCTS YOU ARE EVER LIKELY TO WANT ... OR NEED

A great deal of fuss is made about the huge variety of financial products available on the market but, at the end of the day, there are really only three different areas you need to consider:

1. Lending products;

2. Investment products; and

3. Protection products.

In part two of this book we will examine each of these categories in greater detail. For the time being, however, a quick summary will suffice.

**MONEY DOCTOR WEALTH CHECK**

*The right product at the right price*
It is often said that the biggest purchase most people make is their home. Not true! The biggest purchase most people make is their mortgage! In fact, over the course of your life you could well spend more money on financial products than on

anything else. For this reason it is extremely important to make sure that you buy the right product at the right price. All the more so as financial products may be with you for, literally, decades. Finally, *never* believe that you owe any particular financial institution your loyalty. You can be certain they won't be loyal to you. Always buy the best product for your needs at the lowest possible price. *Never be afraid to shop around.*

## Borrowing products — made easy

Although there are any number of ways to borrow, from credit cards to personal loans and from mortgages to hire purchase, all borrowing falls into one of two types. There's *secured* borrowing and *unsecured* borrowing. The difference is simple. If a loan is secured, and you fail to keep up with the repayments, then the lender is entitled to take an agreed item belonging to you instead. The most obvious example is that of a mortgage on a house. If you fail to make your mortgage repayments then the lender can force the sale of the house and hold on to any money owed to them after the sale.

## All loans are not equal

The greater the security, the lower the interest rate you should have to pay. This is why secured loans are almost always less expensive than unsecured loans. Mortgages are, of course, pretty much the cheapest way to borrow. From a lender's point of view, you can't beat property when it comes to security.

## *Home loans*

There are many sorts of home loans, or mortgages, on the market. The most common of these are:

- *Repayment or annuity mortgages.* With this type of loan your monthly payment is made up of two elements — interest on the total amount you owe plus some of the capital you originally borrowed.

- *Interest-only mortgages* are gaining popularity in the current economic environment. With this type of loan you pay the lender the interest on the amount you owe, but you don't have to repay the capital until the end of the term, typically twenty five years, though they can last for up to forty years. During the term of the loan you are normally, but not always, expected to invest additional money in order to build up a lump sum of capital to pay the whole amount off at the end of the term. Borrowers can use different sorts of investment vehicles to pay off their interest-only mortgages, including endowment insurance policies and pension plans.

In the early 1990s, interest-only loans went out of fashion because many borrowers were sold endowment insurance policies which failed to provide enough capital to repay their original loan at the end of the term. However, for some people, especially property investors, they do make sound sense as they maximise the tax relief against rental income from the constant loan interest that is eligible for offset; as you are not paying back capital the interest never decreases. Recently, interest-only mortgages without any savings or investment element have become popular. These are discussed at some length in Chapter 9.

- *Current account mortgages.* In the recent past and

following the lead from UK lenders, one Irish lender has introduced the *current account mortgage* here. This links your current account to your home loan. If you are good at managing your money this can result in substantial savings. For greater details of this type of mortgage see Chapter 9. However, to save the greatest amount of money, and to become debt-free in the fastest possible time, what you should do is overpay your mortgage each month. Not all lenders allow this (and it isn't possible with a fixed-rate loan) but where it is possible the effect can be dramatic. Of course, once your home loan is in variable interest rate mode, lump sums may be repaid against the loan without any penalty. It may, therefore, be easier to build up savings to a certain level and pay off at that point.

A normal €200,000 mortgage lasting 25 years at an interest rate of 3.25% would cost you around €974.63 a month. If you increased your monthly payment by €400 (or paid a lump sum of €5,000 at the start of each subsequent year) you would own your home outright after just 15 years and you'd save nearly €20,000 in interest.

Finally, the competitiveness of the home loan market now means that if you shop around you can save a huge amount of money. A 1% saving on a €200,000 25-year mortgage from 4% to 3% is worth €32,175 straight into your pocket over the term.

### Other loans

Other loans available include:

- Personal loans
- Overdrafts

- Secured loans
- Asset backed finance
- Credit cards
- Store cards
- Hire purchase
- Credit Union loans

You'll find full details in Chapter 10.

## Good debt ... and bad debt

In my opinion there is good debt and bad debt. Most of us would never be able to buy our own homes without a mortgage. By the same token, money borrowed for such things as education, a car to get you to and from work, or to start your own business obviously makes sense. However, some loans are very bad news. They are expensive and structured in such a way as to make them difficult to pay off. This is discussed further in Chapter 8.

## Saving and investment products — made easy

The less risk lenders have to take, the less they should charge you for borrowing. By the same token, the less risk you take as an investor, the less return you can expect to make.

Thus, if you leave your money in a totally secure bank account you will receive a much lower return than you *could* earn investing it in a riskier proposition.

Savers should have the following broad objectives:

- To build up an emergency fund equal to between three and six months' expenditure. This should be kept where you can get your hands on it relatively easily. You may like to keep a little extra cash on hand too, so that you have money available for investment opportunities, capital expenditure or to pay for some luxury item such as a holiday;

- To start a pension and make sure it is properly funded. This is because the sooner you start (thanks to compound interest and the various tax breaks) the less it will cost you in real terms *and* because ensuring you have a comfortable retirement is crucial;
- To save up money required for important purchases, such as the deposit with which to buy a home;
- To invest for any long-term requirements, such as private education for your children; and
- To build up capital wealth over the long term.

Your emergency fund needs to be in cash and somewhere totally risk-free such as a credit union or deposit account. For your pension it makes sense to use one of the specialist pension products on the market and to take advantage of the extra tax breaks given to those investing for their retirement. But what about the rest of your saving? The secret to successful investment is diversification. You should split your savings across low, medium and higher risk types of investment, with the emphasis being on the low-to-medium risk products. By diversifying in this way you optimise your potential for gain, without having to take a substantial risk.

Here are just some of the saving and investment products you will want to consider:

- Bank, building society and credit union savings and investment accounts
- Gilts and bonds
- Annuities

- Insurance company income and growth bonds
- Corporate bonds
- Preference shares
- Pooled investments such as with-profits life insurance and unit trusts
- Guaranteed equity bonds
- Ordinary shares
- Investment trusts
- BES schemes
- Real Estate Investment Trusts (REITs) — brought into the UK mid-2004.
- Property Investment Funds (introduced in the UK March 2004 Budget)

These products are discussed further in Chapter 14 and Chapter 15.


## Protecting yourself, your family and your possessions — made easy

Because many people don't like thinking about insurance they end up with:

- Too much cover.
- Too little cover.
- The wrong sort of cover.
- Over-priced cover.

Having the wrong (or useless) cover is almost as bad as having no cover at all. It is also possible to waste a lot of money on insurance that would be better spent on, say, paying off your mortgage or a pension. For these reasons I believe it is vital to:

- Concentrate on insurance that you really need; and

- Check the price on a regular basis in case you could be saving money.

Below is a brief summary of the four most important types of insurance:

*Income Protection.* This is known as PHI — permanent health insurance. There are various other policies designed to replace your income, or pay your bills for you, if you can't work due to an accident, illness or, in some cases, redundancy and insolvency. (Note that repayment protector insurance only pays the first 12 months of your mortgage, after which you are on your own!) If you don't have an emergency fund, and especially if you have any debts (including a mortgage), this cover is of equal if not greater value than life cover.

*Life Insurance.* Pays out a lump sum if the insured dies or is killed. Obviously a priority for anyone with dependents. The cost can be reduced by taking out term or even decreasing term (where the cover drops every year) insurance. Where cover is linked to a pension there can be worthwhile tax savings.

*Private Medical Insurance.* Covers the cost of private medical care. More valuable to those who work for themselves as it means no waiting for treatment. The two main providers of private medical insurance in Ireland at the moment are VHI and BUPA.

*General Insurance.* If you own any major item, such as a house or a boat, then clearly you should insure it if its loss would have an impact on your financial position.

See Chapter 11 and Chapter 12 for information about buying insurance.

*The Money Doctor says ...*

- In order to strengthen your financial position it is important to understand the range of financial products available to you.

- All the products discussed in this chapter will be re-examined in much greater detail later in the book.

- The wrong financial product, whether it is a credit card or an over-priced mortgage, can cost you a great deal of money. Make sure you have the right products at the best possible price.

- Every financial decision deserves careful consideration and it is always worth taking independent professional advice.

# 7

# GETTING HELP

## WHO YOU CAN REALLY TRUST TO GIVE YOU THE BEST POSSIBLE ADVICE

Are you the sort of person who relishes the challenge of managing their own financial welfare? Or are you the sort of person who would feel happier passing the whole task to someone else? Either way, this chapter will give you the inside word on:

- Which tasks you should definitely undertake yourself.
- Who you can trust to give you really first class advice.
- How to judge whether a professional adviser is any good.
- Which advisers to avoid like the plague.

## How far should you go?

You want to make the most of your money. In practical terms this means:

- Keeping the cost of your borrowing (including your mortgage) to a bare minimum and making sure you have the most suitable mortgage for your needs;
- Earning the highest possible return from your savings and investments without taking undue risk or paying unnecessary fees or commission;
- Obtaining the best possible pension plan;
- Taking out only the most appropriate insurance at the lowest possible price;
- Not paying a penny more tax than you have to;

- Not paying a penny more for any other financial services or products than you have to; and
- Not being caught by any unscrupulous operators.

With the help of this book, and my web site — *www.moneydoctor.ie* you will certainly be able to achieve all of the above by yourself. However, does the DIY approach make sense for you? The following questions may help you to decide:

*Have you got the right temperament?* Financial planning can be stressful and time consuming. If you hate figure work, don't like making decisions and worry about taking risks then maybe you would be better seeking professional assistance.

*Do you have the time?* Are you willing to give up a few hours a month to make sure you are optimising your finances? Do you see this as being quite good fun? If not, then maybe the DIY approach isn't best for you.

*Can you access the information you need?* Financial planning requires access to information. If you can't gain access to the web, and if you aren't near a good library, then you should possibly let someone else do the legwork for you.

**MONEY DOCTOR WEALTH WARNING**

*Some things are best not delegated*

There is an enormous amount to be said for getting a really good professional adviser to sort out everything for you. You'll save money. You'll save time. And you will end up with the best possible products for your needs. But no matter how good your adviser you should always take time to:

- Understand what he or she is proposing, and why;

- Learn about the products you are committing to; and

- Check up on the financial institutions who will be supplying those products.

You'll find a list of questions to ask your financial adviser at the end of this chapter.

## What help is available?

There are any number of people who would like to help you with your personal finances, from bank managers to life insurance salesmen and from credit brokers to pension specialists. The golden rule is:

The fewer options the 'expert' can offer you, the less you should trust them.

Let me give you one pertinent example. If you go to your bank and express an interest in taking out a pension, whoever you speak to will be duty-bound to sell you something from the bank's own range of products if they have their own tied agency, even if he or she knows you would get a better deal elsewhere. If, on the other hand, you go to an independent financial adviser (an Authorised Advisor) he or she *must* recommend the best and most competitively priced product for your needs, because by virtue of their status as Authorised Advisor, they MUST give 'best advice'.

With regard to mortgage advice, only seek this from advisers who *formally* represent ALL the lenders operating in Ireland (you can check this from the advisers' *Terms of Business* which they MUST give you at your first interview and which lists all their appointments with the product providers), or an adviser to whom you are prepared to pay a fee for such advice, which *should* ensure independence.

No matter how nice someone is, no matter what your experience of dealing with them, the only advice you can trust when it comes to money is that which is *totally independent.* The advice you receive must be from unbiased, impartial, qualified experts. *Accept no substitute!*

**MONEY DOCTOR WEALTH WARNING**

*Convenience costs you*
There is an increasing trend for non-financial institutions and companies to offer financial products. A car dealer will sell you a car loan, a supermarket will offer you a savings plan, and a publisher will sell you home insurance. As a general rule these products tend to be of the 'one size fits all' variety and may not represent very good value for money. Never buy a financial product because it is convenient ... invariably it will end up costing you.

## Dealing with a genuine professional

In order to make sure that consumers receive reliable and independent advice the government set up the Irish Financial

Services Regulatory Authority (IFSRA). One of the first things to do when considering any professional adviser is to check:

1. That they are regulated by the IFSRA; and

2. What services they are authorised to provide and at what cost. They MUST give you a *Terms of Business* booklet which outlines their terms of business, appointments with product providers, IFSRA authorisation and notification of the *Investors' Compensation Act*. (See an example of a Terms of Business booklet in Appendix 3.)

You should only deal with an adviser authorised to provide insurance, investment and credit services. This will mean that they are legally obliged to provide you with the best possible or most appropriate advice.

You can be certain that any individual or firm who *is* authorised will not only have had to pass a stringent series of tests to qualify but that their performance will be strictly monitored on an ongoing basis.

Prior to November 2001 there were over 9,000 'insurance brokers' offering financial advice. The Central Bank took over regulation and forced them to register. 6,000 immediately dropped out and of the two new authorisations available, there are currently around 500 *Authorised Advisors*, who MUST give 'best advice' irrespective of agencies held. The balance of about 2,500 are called *Multi-Agency Intermediaries* (originally called RAIPIs, then *Restricted Intermediaries*, they can only give advice on the insurance and investment appointments held).

Good news for consumers though!

You should be aware that there are a number of professional bodies covering the financial services industry. My own belief is that you should only deal with members of *all* these bodies. These are:

The Independent Mortgage Advisers Federation (IMAF).

The Irish Brokers Association (IBA).

Professional Insurance Brokers Association (PIBA).

Life Insurance Association (LIA).

Your financial adviser should ideally be a QFA, or Qualified Financial Adviser, as well as having substantial financial experience. Individual membership of other professional bodies, such as the Institute of Bankers in Ireland, is also desirable.

Finally, if you are looking for advice on buying company shares then you should deal with intermediaries who are members of (or affiliated members of) the Irish Stock Exchange.

*Don't allow yourself to be tricked into accepting advice from someone who isn't both independent and qualified. At the end of this chapter is a list of questions to ask anyone offering you financial advice. If in doubt visit my web site — www.moneydoctor.ie — for further details. For instance, an Authorised Advisor and Mortgage Intermediary will always insist on:*

- *Conducting a full 'fact find' (see Appendix 2) to make sure they understand your financial position and needs; and*

- *Providing you with a formal Terms of Business booklet (see Appendix 3).*

# What can you expect from your independent professional Authorised Advisor and Mortgage Intermediary?

One of the key advantages to appointing an Authorised Advisor and Mortgage Intermediary, that is to say someone who is independent, professional, qualified and stringently regulated, is that they owe their allegiance *to you* and not to any particular financial institution. It is *your* needs that will be paramount. As a result you can expect them to provide you with the following services:

- *Strategic planning.* Looking at your complete financial position, to agree your financial objectives with you, and advise you on how to reach your money targets. When doing this he or she should also assess your existing position and review any financial products you have in place to make sure they meet your requirements.
- *Competitor analysis.* Having decided what products you need, your adviser should search the market for the best product offering the best value for money.
- *Negotiation services.* When a bank quotes a mortgage rate it isn't necessarily fixed in stone. In fact, it is possible to negotiate discounts on a huge range of financial products. Your adviser will know what else is available in the market and should negotiate to get you the best possible deal.
- *Background information.* Your adviser should provide you with background information on any products or companies they are recommending.
- *Administration.* Your adviser should deal with all the paper-work on your behalf and will assist with the filling out of any forms.
- *Regular reviews.* Your adviser should monitor your needs without being asked. They should constantly be thinking

about your situation and making sure that whatever they have recommended is performing in the desired manner.

Your adviser should be able to look after *all* your financial and money needs, including:

- Mortgages.
- Re-finance.
- Commercial loans.
- Personal loans.
- Asset finance and leasing.
- Life cover.
- Income protection and other insurance.
- Health cover.
- All savings and investments.
- Pensions.
- Property and other general insurance.

Where even more specialised advice is needed, say in the selection of shares to build a portfolio, then your adviser should be able to recommend other professional experts.

## Saving tax

A first-class financial adviser will be able to advise you on tax-saving products. You should bear in mind though that for specialist tax advice you should always go to an accountant or qualified tax consultant. If the size of your business doesn't warrant appointing an accountant, then your financial adviser should still be able to assist you. Tax is a big part of financial planning. After all, what's the point of making a better return on your investments, only to lose it through poor tax advice? You should always check that your adviser is taking your tax position into account and is properly qualified to assist you.

## MONEY DOCTOR WEALTH CHECK

*How financial institutions make their money*
Financial institutions will make money from you in one of four ways:

1. *Fees.* A bank will normally charge a fee for maintaining your current account or for paying standing orders and accepting direct debits on your behalf.

2. *Commission.* A bank selling travellers cheques will charge you a percentage of their face value as commission.

3. *Interest.* A credit card company will charge you interest on the money you owe them.

4. *On the 'spread'.* A bureau de change buying and selling foreign exchange will buy, say, dollars at one price, add in their profit, and sell them on at a higher price.

Depending on the size of your transaction, most especially with a mortgage, *for someone in the know* it may well be possible to negotiate a better deal. This is where financial advisers can sometimes make the difference.

(Note: insurance companies also make their money in a slightly different way: assessing a risk and charging accordingly.)

## How to get the best professional advice there is ... for FREE!

Independent professional financial advisers — Authorised Advisors and Mortgage Intermediaries — make their money in one of two ways:

1. They charge an hourly or flat fee

   and/or

2. They earn commission from the financial institutions whose products they recommend, should the client then subsequently opt for one or more of those products.

From time to time you may see articles in the newspapers suggesting that you shouldn't use a financial adviser on a commission basis because the commission may influence the adviser's recommendations.

*This is absolute nonsense.*

Firstly, an independent professional financial adviser — an Authorised Advisor — MUST be just that: *independent, professional,* and MUST give 'best advice'. They are legally bound to give you the best advice on investments or insurance whether or not they make any commission. If the best advice is that you put your money in An Post or go to a credit union (neither of whom pay commission to advisers) your adviser *must* inform you of this. If he or she doesn't, they risk being put out of business by the Irish Financial Services Regulatory Authority (IFSRA — who took over the regulation from the Central Bank on 1 May 2003). You can rest assured that no professional adviser is ever going to risk his or her reputation (and thus their career) for the sake of a tiny amount of commission.

With regard to the Mortgage Intermediary, choosing one that maintains *all* the lending agencies means that there is no bias. Commission for mortgage introductions paid by the various financial institutions is virtually identical. That adviser therefore will not, in my view, jeopardise his/her reputation, integrity and professionalism, not to mention future referrals, by trying to persuade a client to opt for a product that may be more remunerative to the adviser. It doesn't make sense and it would be very short-sighted.

Secondly, commission is built into the cost of most products even when they are sold direct by the financial institution. A mortgage provider, for instance, will expect to pay commission to an adviser introducing business. However, they won't pay the commission to anyone else. So, by not going this route you are missing an opportunity to receive the best possible financial advice *without obligation* and, even better, *without cost.*

*Please note some independent financial advisers will not take on new clients without a small, refundable, up-front fee or deposit. This is to ensure that the client is committed to the process.*

---

### *The Money Doctor says …*

Here are the questions you should ask any financial adviser before you appoint them:

- Is your firm regulated by the Irish Financial Services Regulatory Authority (IFSRA)? Are you regulated as an Authorised Advisor and a Mortgage Intermediary?
- Which services are you authorised to supply? Ask for their *Terms of Business* to check their agencies.

- Is your firm a member of the following associations and institutes?
  The Independent Mortgage Advisers Federation.
  The Irish Brokers Association.
  Professional Insurance Brokers Association.
  Life Insurance Association.
- Are you a member of the Institute of Bankers or other such body? Are you a QFA (Qualified Financial Adviser)?
- How many years have you been in the financial services industry? (Anything less than fifteen years would suggest too little experience).
- Can your firm provide advice on the following products?
  Mortgages.
  Refinance.
  Commercial loans.
  Personal loans.
  Asset finance and leasing.
  Life cover.
  Income protection and other insurance.
  Health cover.
  All savings and investments.
  Pensions.
  Property insurance.
- Will your firm be able to show me how to reduce my tax bill?
- Will your firm be able to provide the following?
  Strategic planning.
  Market analysis.
  Negotiation services.
  Background information.
  Administration.

> Regular reviews.
> - How many financial institutions does your firm check with when looking for a property loan on behalf of a client? (This is a trick question! At the time of going to press there are 13 providers of property loans in Ireland and your adviser should automatically check with all of them or at least know what is available).
> - How will you expect to be paid for the advice you offer me?

## A word about 'intermediaries'

In the course of your financial travels you may come across 'single-agency' and 'multi-agency' intermediaries. Both are authorised by the IFSRA.

Single-agency intermediaries and 'tied' agents only represent one supplier. In other words, they can't offer you a choice.

Multi-agency intermediaries must hold agencies for at least two product providers. They can only offer and advise you on products for which they have an agency.

*You will have gathered that the Money Doctor does not believe in anything other than Authorised Advisors and Mortgage Intermediaries who represent ALL the lenders operating in Ireland. Going outside these types of advisers severely limits your choice and thus your chances of getting the best products and most appropriate advice for your needs at the best price.*

*The Money Doctor says ...*

- It is possible to handle all your financial decisions without reference to anyone else. However, it requires time and commitment.

- If you do decide to use a professional adviser make sure that they are fully authorised and don't be shy about asking them questions.

- Remember, it is important to have clear financial objectives.

# *8*

## THE JOY OF BEING DEBT-FREE

### WHY IT IS IMPORTANT TO BE DEBT-FREE PLUS HOW TO PAY OFF ALL YOUR DEBTS, INCLUDING YOUR MORTGAGE, QUICKLY AND EASILY

This chapter is devoted to a very important subject: paying off all your debts.

- You don't have to be in any sort of financial difficulty to be in debt.
- When you add up the cost of servicing your debt, including your mortgage, it may come to more than you imagine.
- Debt is the single greatest threat to your financial freedom and security. It is sucking away your most valuable asset: your income.
- The first benefit of being debt-free is that your money becomes your own to spend or invest as you prefer.
- Not having any debt will make you less vulnerable. You won't need so much insurance, for instance.

Paying back all the money you owe, including anything you may have borrowed to buy or improve your home, quickly and easily, is only a matter of following the Money Doctor's proven formula.

### Sizing up the problem

Over the last twenty to thirty years consumer debt has increased at a frightening pace. Why should this be? Some borrowing is unavoidable, such as loans taken out when ill or unemployed. Some can be attributed to other factors such as changing social values, lack of education at school, our consumer society and impulse spending. However, I believe the main reason for the borrowing boom is that debt has become a hugely profitable business. Bluntly, lenders are using clever marketing tricks to push debt on to innocent consumers. They are doing this because the returns are irresistible. Look how much money they can make:

> If you leave money on deposit at a bank you'll typically earn in the region of 1% (€1 for every €100) a year by way of interest.

> That bank, however, can lend your money to someone else at anything up to 19% (€19 for every €100) a year.

Under the circumstances, is it any wonder that financial institutions are falling over themselves to lend money? Or that they devote themselves to coming up with new ways to sell loans to their customers?

## Debt comes in many disguises

The trouble with the word 'debt' is that it has all sorts of negative connotations. Many people believe that providing they are never behind on their repayments, they are not in debt. This isn't true. A debt is when you owe someone money. It could be:

- An unpaid balance on a credit card.
- An overdraft.
- A personal loan.
- A car loan or loan for some other specific purchase.
- A mortgage on your home.

- A secured loan.
- A hire purchase agreement.
- An unpaid balance on a store charge card.
- A business loan.
- A loan made by a friend or family member.

It is important to remember that just because you are never in arrears and have an excellent credit rating, it doesn't mean that you are debt-free.

## The true cost of debt

In Chapter 2 I explained how compound interest can boost your wealth. However, compound interest can also cost you dear. Refer to my example of the person who borrows €5,000 on a credit card at a rate of 15% per annum and repays the bare minimum of 1.5% per month. Because the interest you pay on your debt is attracting even more interest the example clearly shows the insidious effect of compounding.

The truth is that you make your lender happy when you:

- Borrow as much as possible;
- Pay it back over as long a period as possible;
- Borrow at the highest possible interest rate; and
- Make the minimum monthly payment.

You should be particularly wary of the 'minimum payment trap', where the lender allows you to pay back very little of the debt each month. This is particularly prevalent in the credit card and store card sector. When you opt for the minimum monthly repayment, your repayment will be made up almost completely of interest so that the debt itself hardly ever gets reduced. Another thing to watch for is 'revolving credit' — where you can keep topping up the loan to its original level or where the lender keeps upping your credit limit or offering you new loans.

## Debt threatens your future freedom

I wouldn't go so far as to say that all debt is bad. There are plenty of instances where borrowing money makes financial sense, in order to buy your own home, for example, or to pay for education. It is when you are borrowing money to finance your lifestyle that you are getting into dangerous territory. Living beyond your means threatens your future financial freedom. Let me give you an example:

Cathal is the manager of a supermarket and earns a good income. However, it isn't enough to cover all the things he and his family like to enjoy, so he frequently borrows. In a typical year he might borrow to pay for Christmas presents, a holiday, or just to cover other shortfalls in his monthly expenditure such as clothes or eating out. He views this as short-term debt, but the reality is that every year between the ages of 35 and 55 he borrows an average of €4,000 more than he earns. Because this is short-term, unsecured debt he pays an average of 12% a year in interest. His monthly debt repayments (excluding his mortgage) are €360.

Cathal's twin brother, Ray, is also a supermarket manager and earns exactly the same income. However, he lives within his means. He doesn't eat out as often, go on holiday as frequently or drive such a nice car. He saves the €360 his brother spends each month on servicing his debts and instead he invests the money. He manages a return of 6% a year between the ages of 35 and 55 and so he builds up a tax-free lump sum of €160,000.

The fact is that your most valuable asset is your income and there is only so much that each of us will ever earn during our lifetimes. By spending a large portion of it on servicing debt you are, basically, giving it away to your lenders. Surely your need is greater than theirs?

## Seven excellent reasons to become debt-free

Here are seven reasons why you should pay off all your debts, including, perhaps, your mortgage:

1. It will make you less vulnerable. If you are in debt and for some reason your income is reduced or stops altogether (suppose, for instance you fall seriously ill and don't have permanent health insurance or serious illness cover) then not being able to repay your loans could have serious consequences;
2. It will make your family less vulnerable. I don't want to depress you but when you die your debts won't die with you — your estate will have to pay them all;
3. You won't have to worry about inflation. If you owe money and interest rates rise (as recently as 1991 interest rates were as high as 19%) then you could easily find yourself struggling to make your monthly payments;
4. You won't have the stress which comes with debt. The fact is that owing money is stressful;
5. You'll enjoy a genuine sense of satisfaction. There is a real peace of mind which comes with not owing money and owning your home outright;
6. It will open up new choices. Suddenly all the money you are spending on servicing your debts will be available for you to spend or save as you prefer; and
7. It will ensure you have a comfortable retirement. Furthermore, it may allow you to retire early. Why should you have to wait until you are 60 or 65 to give up work?

## MONEY DOCTOR WEALTH WARNING

*How lenders will try to trick you*

With so much profit at stake, lenders put a lot of effort into persuading consumers to borrow. There is a catch to every offer! Let me give you an example:

> Josephine goes to buy a new bed in the Red-Ted sale. It is marked down from €1300 to €1100 and as she goes to pay, the shop assistant persuades her to take out a Red-Ted Store Card as it will give her an extra discount. So instead of €1100 she pays just €1000. However, Josephine doesn't pay off her store card at the end of the month but instead takes 36 months to do so. The result? Because she is being charged 15% interest the bed ends up costing her €1248. Not so much of a saving, after all.

A couple of other things to watch out for: Firstly, loan consolidation. When used properly — as I will explain in a moment — loan consolidation is an excellent way to speed yourself out of debt. However, unscrupulous lenders often lure borrowers into taking out expensive consolidation loans, even encouraging them to borrow extra for a holiday or other luxury item. Secondly, transferring credit card debt to save money. Only too often a low interest or zero interest period is followed by a much higher rate. Check the conditions carefully and don't be taken in by lenders.

## Why NOW is an excellent time to pay off all your debts

At the moment we are lucky enough to be in what economists call a low-interest-rate environment. In fact, interest rates have not been as low in living memory. Instead of using this as an excuse to borrow more, the sensible thing to do is to take advantage of the cheap cost of money to repay all your debts.

## The first step to getting out of debt

There is one thing you must do before you set out to eradicate all your debt: stop borrowing. After all, you can't get yourself out of a hole if you keep digging. Take a once-and-for-all decision to:

- Not just to pay off your debts, but to stay out of debt;
- Not to borrow any more money unless it is absolutely unavoidable (or there is a very reasonable chance that you can invest the money you borrow to make more than the loan is going to cost you to repay);
- Not to live beyond your means; and
- Avoid 'Bargains'. In my book a genuine bargain is something you need to buy but which you manage to get at a price lower than you expected to pay for it. Something that you don't need but you buy because it seems to be cheap is definitely not a bargain.

There are various actions you can take to make this easier on yourself, including:

- Cutting up all your credit cards and store cards;
- Cancelling your overdraft limit;

- Using a charge card where the balance has to be paid in full at the end of each month;
- Not buying any unnecessary items;
- Not taking out any new loans including hire purchase agreements and overdrafts;
- Not increasing the size of any existing loans; and
- Paying with cash whenever possible (nothing reduces one's tendency to spend money as paying with cash).

There is an American money expert called Alvin Hall who you may have seen on television. For anyone who has trouble curbing their expenditure he suggests keeping what he calls a 'money diary'. The basic idea is that you carry a small notebook with you wherever you go and write down details of · every single penny you spend. You should include everything from your daily newspaper to your mortgage repayments. After a couple of weeks you'll have a precise picture of where your money is going and this, in turn, will help you avoid spending money on things you don't really want or need. If you are prone to impulse spending or if you always spend more than your income I can see the good sense in this approach.

## Taking stock of your situation

Once you have stopped making the situation any worse you need to take stock of your situation. In particular, you want to gather together full details of your debts. The information you require about each of your debts is:

- To whom you owe the money;
- How big the debt is;
- How long you have to pay it back (the term), if relevant;

- What the rate of interest is and whether it is fixed or variable;
- Whether you will be penalised for paying back the debt early (and if so what the penalties are);
- What the minimum monthly payment is (if this is relevant); and
- Whether the interest is calculated daily, monthly or annually.

Obviously, it is important not to overlook any possible debts, so here is a quick checklist to remind you. Don't forget to include any money that your spouse or partner may owe, too!

Mortgages
Secured loans
Credit cards
Store cards
Overdrafts
Personal loans
Car loans
Hire or lease purchase agreements
Catalogue company loans
Family or friends who may have lent you money
Student loans

Most of the information you need should be supplied to you each month by your lenders. However, if it isn't, then you should telephone or write to them asking for full details.

## The 'savings' conundrum

One situation the Money Doctor often encounters is of 'patients' who have debts BUT who are saving money at the same time.

In most cases it makes sense to stop saving money and to use any existing savings to pay off some or all of your debts. Why? Because usually what you are earning from your savings will be substantially less than what you are paying out to borrow.

€100 in a savings account may be earning you as little as 50 cent per annum after tax.

€100 owed on, say, a credit card may be costing you as much as €19 or more a year.

So, if you had savings of €1000 and used it to pay off €1000 of credit card debt you could be saving yourself as much as €190 a year. More, as much as €240 a year, if you have borrowed on a store card.

Where it may not make sense to cash in your savings is if you have one of the government's Special Savings Incentive Accounts.

In the case of endowment policies it will depend on the policy. You would be well advised to take professional advice since some are worth more than others.

Overall, however, it does not make financial sense to be investing a small amount of money each month if, at the same time, you are spending a small fortune on servicing a debt.

## The art of debt elimination

You've taken the decision not to incur any extra debt. You've got a real grip on the size and nature of your problem. What next? You have two options:

## *Option One: The consolidation approach*

The idea behind consolidation is to dramatically reduce the cost of your debt. Instead of having lots of different loans, all at different rates, you have a single loan at one, much lower rate. It works particularly well if you own your own home. What you do is:

• Add up all the money you currently spend making your debt repayments;

• Consolidate all your debts into a single, much cheaper loan; and

• Keep on making the same monthly payments.

This is best explained with an example. Below I have listed off all the debts that Brian and Sheila have, along with the interest rate they are paying on each one:

| Type of debt | Monthly cost | Interest rate |
| --- | --- | --- |
| Mortgage | €800 | 4% |
| Home improvement loan | €16 | 10% |
| Credit card 1 | €45 | 16% |
| Credit card 2 | €30 | 16% |
| Store card | €71 | 17% |
| Car loan | €225 | 10% |

The total amount Brian and Sheila are spending on their debts is €1,337 a month. Since they own their own home they can consolidate all their debts in with their mortgage. At the moment their mortgage is for €128,000 and has 19 years to run. Although consolidating their loans increases their mortgage to €152,000, by continuing to pay €1,200 a month they can shorten the length of their mortgage to just 14 years. At the same time they will save themselves €18,500 in interest! Incidentally, to optimise the benefit of consolidation, it may be preferable to take out something called a current account mortgage. The full benefits of these mortgages are explained in Chapter 9.

Please remember debt consolidation should be a once-in-a-lifetime course of action. It only works to your advantage if you carry on making the same or lower monthly payments. Otherwise all you are doing is spreading the cost of your short-term debt over the longer term. I believe one should never borrow money for a longer period than the life of the asset you are buying, unless it is to fund a major capital expense on a once-off basis e.g. buying a brand new expensive car but then using savings over the next three years to fund the next car purchase. However, if the purpose of the consolidation is to increase your cash flow and allow you to live a half-decent life, it may well be the more prudent option to take.

## Option Two: The Sniper Approach

If you don't own your own home, or if you don't have sufficient capital tied up in your property to consolidate your debts in with your mortgage, you'll need to take what I call the 'sniper' approach. This involves 'picking off' your debts one at a time, starting with the most expensive. What you do is:

- Find some extra money. Just because you don't have a mortgage doesn't mean that you can't consolidate your debt. Move your borrowing to where it is costing you the least; and
- Use the money you are saving each month to pay off your most expensive debt, in other words the one with the highest rate of interest.

Do you sometimes pay more than the minimum amount required each month? If you do, then make sure you pay it towards whichever of your debts is costing you the most. Incidentally, you may find that one or more of your existing lenders will be open to negotiation.

To use a typical example, imagine that Neil has the following debts:

| Type of debt | Monthly/minimum cost | Interest rate |
|---|---|---|
| Credit card €4,000 | €60 | 16% |
| Store card €5,000 | €75 | 17% |
| Car loan €8,000 | €258 | 10% |

Every month he usually pays about €100 more off one or other of the debts on a purely random basis. Also, he is able to find €100 from other sources to help speed himself out of debt. In other words, Neil has €200 extra to apply to getting himself out of debt. Therefore what he needs to do is pay off his most expensive debt first — his store card. By paying an extra €200 a month he can do this within 20 months. This frees up the store card minimum payment of €75 to help pay off his next most expensive debt, which is his credit card.

## MONEY DOCTOR WEALTH CHECK

*Put your money to the best possible use ...*
The secret to getting rid of your debts is putting your money to the best possible use. Your objective

is to get your loans onto the lowest possible rate of interest and then to use the saving to speed up the process of paying off your debt.

Of course, if you could find some extra money each month then you could get out of debt even faster. One way to find extra money is to look at the way you spend your income and see if you can make some basic savings without necessarily cutting back. For example:

- Many people pay more than they have to for their banking. Review your arrangements. Could you be earning extra interest? Saving interest? Avoiding unnecessary costs like surcharge fees for going over your overdraft?
- Don't pay for anything you neither need nor use, such as membership fees, internet charges and magazines.
- Double check you aren't overpaying your tax. Is your code correct?
- Review all your insurance costs. This is a fiercely competitive market and you may be able to save a substantial amount.

In general, it isn't what you earn but how you spend it which will make the difference to your finances. You could be on an enormous salary but if you are up to your neck in debt (as many high income earners are) it is useless to you.

*The Money Doctor says ...*

- If you only take action on one aspect of your finances, make it your priority to get yourself out of debt;

- The first step is to stop borrowing and to get a realistic position of what you owe and how much it is costing you;

- Consider consolidating your debt in with your mortgage. Remember, if you save money or have any spare cash, you should put it towards paying off your debts; and

- Pay your most expensive debts off first.

# PART TWO

# THE PRACTICALITIES OF
# FINANCIAL HEALTH

# 9

## EVERYTHING YOU NEED TO KNOW ABOUT MORTGAGES

### HOW TO CUT THE COST OF YOUR HOME LOAN, PLUS ANSWERS TO ALL YOUR MORTGAGE QUESTIONS

The mortgage maze has become increasingly difficult to negotiate as a growing number of lenders offer an ever-growing range of home loan options. This chapter explains:

- How to take advantage of the demand for your business;
- How to make sure you've got the mortgage that suits you best;
- How to make sure you are paying the lowest possible price; and
- Who to trust for mortgage advice.

Plus we look at how mortgages work, remortgaging, tax relief and just about every other property-related question you can think of.

### Taking advantage of the mortgage revolution

Please put any pre-conceptions you have about buying a home or arranging a mortgage to one side. The truth is:

- Your home is *not* necessarily your most important investment;
- Your home is definitely *not* your most expensive purchase;
- You *don't* have to take 25 years to pay back your mortgage;
- You *aren't* tied to one lender for any longer than you want to be; and

- You *don't* have to move to a different lender to get a better mortgage rate.

Also, and this is crucial to keeping the cost of buying your home or investment property to a bare minimum:

- The interest rate your mortgage lender charges you makes a huge difference to the cost of buying your home; and
- The type of mortgage you have also makes a huge difference to the cost of buying your home.

Over the last few years there has been a mortgage revolution in Ireland. New products and greater competition means there are more opportunities than ever to slash the cost of buying your home — opportunities which no homeowner, or would-be homeowner, should ignore.

## Not necessarily your most important investment — definitely not your most expensive purchase

Received wisdom has it that the most important investment most of us will probably ever make is in our home. There is no doubt that owning your home is a significant part of being financially secure:

- The cost is not dissimilar to renting a home — making it a good financial decision;
- You aren't at the mercy of unscrupulous, unpleasant, greedy or inefficient landlords; and
- With luck you'll see the value of your property rise — giving you a tax-free gain.

Nevertheless, although it makes sense to buy your own home you shouldn't be fooled into thinking that it is the be-all and end-all of investments. It is arguable, in fact, that building up your other investments, especially a pension plan, is substantially more important. Furthermore, the stock market has, traditionally, always produced a better return than property. I'm not trying to put you off buying your own home, *far from it*, but don't forget it is only one part of establishing your personal wealth.

It is also worth remembering that your home won't automatically be your most expensive purchase. Depending on interest rates, that honour could easily go to your mortgage. If you buy a house for €200,000 and take out a traditional, repayment mortgage for €160,000 (80% of the purchase price) and pay it back over 25 years at an average rate of 4%, the total cost of buying your home (including interest) will be €253,362. *That's €53,362 more than the actual cost of your home.* Which is why it is crucial you choose the least expensive mortgage option available to you.

## *Throwing out the traditional mortgage rules*

There was a time, not so long ago, when all mortgages were pretty much the same. Loans lasted for 20 or even 25 years; it was unheard of to pay your mortgage off early; borrowers were discouraged from switching between different lenders; and the lenders themselves would not have dreamt of re-negotiating an existing loan.

All this has changed.

There are currently 13 different financial institutions offering mortgages in Ireland and, thanks to the euro and greater freedom of financial services within Europe, we can look forward to more lenders coming into the market. This means increased competition for your custom, with the result that:

• Better and better deals are available all the time;

- There is much more emphasis on coming up with new, more beneficial home loan products; and
- Lenders are more open to negotiation.

Lenders know that it is now easy to move your mortgage elsewhere, whether or not you are moving your home, and they don't want to lose your business. If you can find a better mortgage deal than the one you are on, you may even find that your existing lender will match it rather than see you re-mortgage elsewhere. A mortgage revolution has taken place and, as a consumer, you'd be crazy not to take advantage of it.

## All the difference in the world

The rate of interest you are charged on your mortgage makes a HUGE difference to the total cost of your home, as the table below indicates:

**Cost of €100,000 — 25 year — repayment mortgage**

| Annual interest rate | Total interest over term |
| --- | --- |
| 3.75% | €54,239 |
| 4% | €58,350 |
| 4.25% | €65,251 |
| 4.5% | €66,750 |
| 4.75% | €71,034 |
| 5% | €75,377 |
| 5.25% | €79,773 |
| 5.5% | €84,225 |
| 5.75% | €88,730 |
| 6% | €93,290 |
| 6.25% | €97,900 |
| 6.5% | €102,561 |
| 6.75% | €107,224 |
| 7% | €112,033 |

The difference between paying, say, 5.5% and 6.5%, which doesn't sound like much, actually equates to €18,336 of interest over the 25 year term. Put another way, think how much extra you would have to earn *after tax* to end up with €18,336 in your pocket. *Paying more mortgage interest than you have to can seriously damage your wealth.* Shopping around makes excellent sense.

## Two mortgage options: repayment versus interest-only

Although there is a whole range of mortgages to choose from, they all fall into one of two categories:

The first option is a *repayment* (or *annuity*) mortgage. With this type of mortgage your monthly repayments are divided into two parts. The first part is the interest you owe on the total amount borrowed. The second part is repayment of part of the capital you have borrowed. The big advantage of this mortgage is that you are guaranteed to have paid off your whole loan at the end of the term. However, in the early years almost all your monthly repayments will be in interest. Let me give you an example:

Sheila takes out a €200,000 mortgage over 25 years at an interest rate of 3.55%. Her monthly capital and interest repayments are €1,006.62. At the end of the first year she will have paid a total of €10,066.20 but will still owe nearly €196,000 to her lender. By year ten she will have paid about €119,000 and will still owe €141,500. Put another way, in the first ten years, two-thirds of what she pays to her lender will be interest, and only one-third will be capital.

## MONEY DOCTOR WEALTH CHECK

*Save extra interest*

When choosing a repayment mortgage make sure interest is calculated daily or at least monthly ('monthly rest'). Why? Because over the term of your mortgage this will save you a tidy sum of money. The real thing to avoid is something called the 'annual rest system', which will cost you the most. Interest is calculated on an annual basis on the balance of your mortgage and added to the mortgage account at the start of the year. Subsequent monthly mortgage repayments do NOT affect the interest. Some lenders still have customers on their books who are on this system and it can add about 0.35% to your interest rate.

The other sort of mortgage on offer is an *interest-only* mortgage. With this type of mortgage you pay only the interest for the agreed period. At the same time you could set up a savings plan which, it would be hoped, would pay off the capital at the end of the term. Your monthly repayments will, therefore, consist of interest on the loan and a contribution to a savings plan.

In the case of an investment property there are circumstances where you might not bother with the savings element, as I'll explain in a moment.

In the past, endowment mortgages got a bad name for themselves because many borrowers were advised to take out insurance policies (see below for an explanation) to repay the capital at the end of the term. Some of these policies failed to produce a sufficient return to do so. In other words, borrowers found that after 25 years they still owed money to their lenders, or the policy was not on course to pay the amount originally borrowed.

Despite past problems with endowment mortgages, they *can* make sound financial sense. For instance, on residential or commercial properties where the investor needs to maximise the highest level of annual interest to offset his or her rental income tax liability, it can have a very tax-efficient effect.

If you are self-employed the tax benefits of a pension-linked interest-only mortgage can also be very substantial.

Here is a quick summary of the three main types of interest-only mortgage options available:

*Endowment mortgages.* Endowment policies are investments offered by life insurance companies. The money you pay to the life insurance company is partly used to provide you with life cover (so that if you die the mortgage itself can be repaid) and partly invested in the stock market. If the money is invested well, then your original loan will be repaid and you might even be left with a tax-free sum. However, if the performance of the endowment policy is not good, then you could be left with insufficient cash to repay your original loan. There are various types of endowment policy available. There is no tax relief available on the endowment policy premiums.

*Pension-linked mortgages.* The difference between this and an endowment mortgage is that the life insurance company (after taking out money to pay for life cover) invest your cash into a pension fund. This has very definite tax benefits for anyone who is self-employed or on an extremely high income. Ordinarily, the pension fund is set to mature on your retirement age at double the original amount borrowed.

25% of that fund at maturity is available for encashment, tax free, and paying tax on the balance of the fund should leave enough to pay off the rest of the mortgage.

New rules on Self-Direct Trusts or SSAPs (Small Self-Administered Pension schemes) now allow pension funds to borrow on properties. The Finance Bill (2004) will allow you to borrow for the first time against your pension fund on a property where the rental income and contributions have tax reliefs available while no capital gains tax liability incurs. This is of course a very complex area, and you would need to have expert advice, including the services of a pensioneer and trustee.

*Interest-only mortgages.* It is now possible to borrow money to purchase property at very competitive rates of interest without any obligation to repay the capital before the end of the term. For instance, if you took out a twenty-year interest-only mortgage, all you have to pay each month is the agreed rate of interest. The capital sum isn't due until twenty years have passed. This could suit you for all sorts of reasons. Perhaps you are expecting to receive a lump sum, such as an inheritance, before the twenty years are up. Maybe you intend to re-sell the property during this period. Possibly you have other investments that could be cashed in to repay the loan. You could even win the Lotto! There is only a slight increase in the cost of your mandatory life cover (if aged under 50) as level term cover must be taken out, ensuring the full sum is insured for the entire term right up to the maturity date.

## Fixed or variable rate?

As if you didn't have enough choice already, another decision to make when mortgage shopping can be whether to opt for a fixed or variable rate.

A fixed rate means that the amount of interest you pay is pre-set for an agreed period of time. This offers you the benefit of certainty. Even if interest rates rise your repayments will stay the same. On the other hand if interest rates fall you won't benefit. You incur a penalty should you wish to pay off or part-pay your mortgage while on a fixed rate of interest. Generally this is set at between three and six months interest on the amount being repaid.

A variable rate, on the other hand, will move with the market. This is fine while interest rates are low but if they begin to rise you could be adversely affected. There is generally no penalty if you wish to pay off all or part of the loan.

One derivation of the variable interest rate is the now very popular *mortgage tracker*. This is where the interest rate offered 'tracks' the European Central Bank (ECB) interest rate plus the lender's margin (agreed at the outset for the entire term) from 0.85% to 1.49%. This margin is the lender's profit and stays constant throughout the mortgage term. Like the variable rate, lump sums may be paid off the home loan at no penalty.

*The Money Doctor says ...*

Unless you are self-employed, on a high income or have some other source of funds coming to you in the future, the Money Doctor normally recommends that you take out a repayment or annuity mortgage when buying your main home. Certain lenders allow either a certain period (one to ten years) or the full term on an interest-only basis, depending on loan-to-value (generally less than 80%), minimum loan being borrowed (in one case, the minimum is €250,000) or whether they are second-time borrowers (again, one lender will not allow interest-only loans to first-time buyers). Generally, this type of loan is ideal for first-time buyers to give themselves a chance to set up the home, get used to paying a mortgage for the first time and have some money left over to enjoy life, so finding the right lender to facilitate this is important!

## A word about 'current account' mortgages

A few years ago, for the first time in decades, a genuinely new and revolutionary mortgage product came onto the market. It is called the *current account* mortgage. At the moment it is only offered by a few institutions in Ireland but, if the market moves here as it has in the UK, then more lenders are likely to provide this option. Essentially, it links your mortgage and current account whereby, on a daily basis, interest is calculated on the balance of the mortgage *minus* the balance of the current account. This has the effect of reducing the accruing interest and, obviously, the higher the balance in your current account the greater is the saving in interest. By opting for a planned repayment schedule, where the monthly repayment is based on the original loan amount, you will both save on interest and reduce the term of the loan.

## A few words about Equity Release products for those in retirement

Many retired people own their own home but find themselves short of cash. One option, in these circumstances, is to sell the home and move to a smaller, less expensive property. Another option is to take advantage of no repayment equity release schemes.

Equity release — which is only available to those aged 65 or over — is a method of unlocking some of the capital from your home without having to move. If you avail of an equity release loan, you won't have to make any repayments either, because the total cost will be met when you eventually sell your home or die. Frankly, it can be an expensive way to raise money and should only be considered after all other options have been explored. The situations where I recommend equity release are when:

- Moving home would cause major inconvenience or stress;
- It doesn't matter that there will be less of an inheritance for the beneficiaries;
- The benefit of cash *now* outweighs the long term cost; and
- You have fully checked out the tax impact on your income by taking out such a loan. Those on non-contributory pensions should seek expert advice.

I am not saying that equity release is overly expensive, just that the costs can mount up.

### Two different types of equity release scheme are available in Ireland for the over-65s.

The *first* is, in essence, a mortgage on your home without any capital or interest repayments whatsoever. Instead the interest is carried forward until the home is sold. As the rate of interest is likely to be both above average and fixed for a long period this can result in a hefty liability. A €200,000 equity release loan would cost you in the region of €400,000 after ten years, assuming an interest rate of, say, 6.75% (one lender offers this product with a mandatory 15-year fixed rate, and the loan is fixed every 15 years until the client/s dies or vacates the home). With no repayments the effect is that the original debt doubles every 10 years but you are entitled to live in your home until you die. Minimum age for this product is 65.

The *second* or alternative method of equity release is to actually sell a share in your home to a company that will allow you to carry on living there until you decide to sell or until you (and your partner, if relevant) die. How much you would get under the circumstances will be linked not just to the value of your home but also to your age, gender and health, as these companies take the interest from the amount sought *upfront*. The downside is that in two of the three schemes, should you die sooner than expected, the company in that case wins out. Minimum age for this type of loan is 70.

For a minority of people, equity release is the ideal way to pay for home nursing care or a necessary home improvement should you wish to remain in your own home. You should *always* take independent professional advice before buying any type of equity release product.

## Why you should try to make mortgage overpayments

Something I have become very keen on in recent years is the idea of overpaying your mortgage each month. This can't be done with all mortgages (for instance, you can't do it where you are on a fixed rate) but where it is possible, the lender allows it and your income allows, it brings real benefits. Consider these two examples:

Mary takes out a repayment mortgage for €250,000 with a term of 30 years at 3.25%. Her monthly repayment is €1,088.02. However, she decides that she can afford to pay an extra €200 a month. As a result, her mortgage will be paid off 7 years earlier and she will save €36,390 in interest.

John also takes out a repayment mortgage for €320,000 with a term of 25 years at 3.55%. His monthly repayment is €1,610.59. He over-pays by €300 a month and, as a result, his mortgage will be paid off 6 years earlier and he will save €42,760 in interest.

In both instances, by taking out a current account mortgage they could save even more interest. This is because any money on deposit in their current account is offset against their mortgage debt.

---

*The Money Doctor says ...*

With so many mortgage choices available many borrowers worry that they are making the right decision for their needs. This is where a really good independent financial adviser can help. He or she will be able to guide you to the least expensive, most appropriate mortgage for your needs. See below for further advice on choosing an adviser.

---

## How a financial adviser will save you money

It goes without saying that you should shop around for the best possible mortgage deal as so much of your hard-earned cash is at stake. Two things to watch out for:

- You may not always be comparing like with like. There is a great deal of difference between a 10-year fixed-rate mortgage and a current account repayment mortgage. Each will cost a different amount and each is designed to meet different needs.
- You may not be offered a full range of options. A bank or building society, for instance, might only have three or four types of mortgage to offer you. Many mortgage advisers deal with less than five lenders. According to a recent survey by the Consumer Association of Ireland more than 86% of the 900 mortgage intermediaries in Ireland have fewer than 5 of the 13 available lending agencies operating in Ireland.

To get the best possible deal you should always deal with an adviser who is *authorised* to act on behalf of every single lender.

There are only a handful of these advisers who act for ALL lenders and, as their fees on home and residential investment loans are paid by the lenders who receive their applications, it means their professional and independent advice will cost you the consumer nothing, other than possibly a refundable fee to commit you to the process.

You may also opt to go to fee-based mortgage advisers where lenders' commissions are refunded to clients should they proceed with those advisers.

Please remember, too, that even if you are a customer with a particular financial institution, an independent adviser may still be able to negotiate a better deal on your behalf. This is because a professional will know what and where the best deal available actually is, while the lender will know that the adviser has other options should the lender fall short of the client's requirement.

> ## MONEY DOCTOR WEALTH CHECK
>
> *The latest information ...*
> If you want the latest financial information —
> everything from interest rates to tax saving tips —
> then log on to my special web site
> *www.moneydoctor.ie*

## Frequently Asked Mortgage Questions

Should I buy or rent my home?

How much can I borrow on my income?

Is it worth switching my mortgage to get a lower rate?

Help! I'm self-employed. How do I get a mortgage?

What will it cost for me to buy my home?

What tax relief will I receive on my home loan?

Does it make sense to buy a second property as an investment?

What are the benefits of owning a home in a designated area?

What's the story with local authority loans?

What other State housing grants might be available to me?

Is it worth repaying my mortgage early?

What different sorts of home insurance will I need?

If I have trouble making my mortgage repayments what should I do?

*Should I buy or rent my home?*
Broadly speaking the cost of buying a home is the same as, or in many cases less than, renting the same property. This is linked to supply and demand, of course, and varies from region to region as well as from property to property. We are in a low-interest environment at the moment, and this favours house purchase, as does the availability of mortgage interest relief. If a future government was to introduce greater tenant rights the situation might change but, at the moment, if you can raise a sufficient deposit, buying makes better long-term sense. After all, when you give up a rental property you receive nothing back, whereas when you have paid off your mortgage you will own your home *and* may have seen a nice, tax-free capital gain as well.

*How much can I borrow on my income?*
You should always put down as much of a deposit as possible when buying your home. You will need a minimum of 8% of the purchase price (that is to say €24,000 if you are buying a €300,000 property) but it is preferable to have more. Why? Because it makes you less vulnerable to moves in interest rates and property values *plus* your financial adviser will be able to negotiate a lower interest rate with a lender if you have over 20% deposit.

Depending on your income, lenders will generally give you a mortgage of three and four-and-a-half times your income. For example:

If you are single and earn €60,000 a year you may be able to borrow up to €270,000 over 35 years.

If you and your partner earn a combined income of €80,000 you may be able to borrow between €300,000 and €350,000 over 35 years.

However, it is always worth remembering that interest rates may rise in the future and if possible you should try and avoid borrowing the maximum amount.

Note: if you are a young professional (e.g. barrister, dentist, accountant, etc.) borrowing money for the first time, you may be able to borrow 100% of the purchase price of your home with certain lenders.

### Is it worth switching my mortgage to get a lower rate?

The short answer is: it depends! Many lenders offer all sorts of exciting inducements to new customers at the expense of their existing borrowers who get charged more. There are two things to consider:

- How much can you save by switching lender?
- What is switching lender going to cost you?

The first question is relatively easy to answer. The second question will depend on a variety of factors including:

- Whether you are on a fixed interest rate, in which case there may be a penalty for breaking the fixed rate contract; and
- How much, if anything, the new lender is going to charge you by way of legal and other costs. Some lenders even offer to pay the legal fees if you switch over to them.

If you can save 0.25% a year interest, or more, it could well be worth the switch. If in doubt, consult an adviser or accountant and ask them to do the figures for you.

### Help! I'm self-employed. How do I get a mortgage?

Most financial institutions are pleased to lend to someone who is self-employed, though if you have less than three years' worth of accounts it may be harder. This is another instance where a professional adviser will help. He or she will know which lenders are keen for your business and willing to offer you the lowest rates.

Note: it is no longer possible to get a mortgage in Ireland without a statement from your accountant to the effect that your tax affairs are completely up to date.

### *What will it cost for me to buy my home?*

There are various expenses involved in buying a home:

- *Survey fees* — each lender has their own valuation panel and MUST obtain a report from the valuer on the property they wish to lend on
- *Indemnity Bond* — most lenders absorb this cost but some still charge their clients the cost of this bond. Once your loan is over 80% and under 92% of the purchase price, the lender takes out an insurance policy that in the event that they have to repossess, sell but do not recoup their loan fully, this policy will pay out the difference down to that 80%. Check with your lender/adviser for details of whether this is applicable to you
- *Stamp duty* on the property (see table on *www.moneydoctor.ie*)
- *Legal fees* generally 1% of price +VAT
- *Outlay* including
  - *Land registry fees*
  - *Search fees*
  - *Stamp duty on the mortgage*

If you would like to know exactly what your mortgage repayments are going to cost, you can visit my web site — *www.moneydoctor.ie* — where you'll find a calculator that will work it out for you.

To give you a typical example, for a first-time buyer purchasing a house for €200,000 with an 80% mortgage (€160,000) the total fees will be in the order of about €9,200, excluding indemnity bond and the deposit (20%).

### *What tax relief will I receive on my home loan?*

You will be entitled to *mortgage interest relief* which will be given to you automatically and called 'tax relief at source' (TRS). See my web site for 'Tax Credits and Allowances' for specific details. There is something called *bridging loan interest relief* (a bridging loan is where you borrow money to buy a new home before you have vacated, but have a contract for sale signed on, your previous home) but, since it is almost impossible to obtain bridging finance in Ireland, this is largely irrelevant. Irish lenders have long stopped 'open-ended bridging' — this is where you buy a new home without having sold your existing home. Lenders will not take the risk of finding that you cannot sell your first home for whatever reason and be left with two major loans. Where you have a contract for sale signed together with a 10% deposit paid on your existing home, this is called 'closed bridging' and lenders can facilitate in these cases, knowing that it takes only a matter of weeks for the purchasers' funds to come through to clear off the bridging facility.

### *Does it make sense to buy a second property as an investment?*

Buying property and renting it out has become an increasingly popular investment over the last few years. There are various reasons for this including:

- Tax incentives. You can claim any loan interest you pay against any rental income you receive *plus* if you buy certain types of property or property in particular areas you will receive additional tax breaks;

- Rapid increases in property values;
- High yields in relation to other investments; and
- Low cost of borrowing money.

In general, the only investors who *don't* make money from renting out property are those who have over-estimated the return they'll receive, haven't allowed for all the likely costs and lack the patience to wait out any market downturns. The secret to success is undoubtedly:

- Allow for periods without tenants (known as 'voids');
- Make sure you have calculated all the costs, including loan repayments, redecoration, maintenance, repair and property management costs; and
- Don't view it as a short-term investment.

### *What are the benefits of owning a home in a designated area?*
If you buy, build or restore a house in particular areas of the country, called designated areas, you are entitled to tax relief on part of the expense. This tax relief is quite generous and well worth claiming. See my web site for a detailed description of the various designated areas and the tax breaks applicable.

### *What's the story with local authority loans?*
County councils and city corporations both provide financial support to anyone on relatively low incomes so that they can afford to buy their own home. This support may come in the form of a mortgage or a mortgage subsidy. They may also buy a house with you on a 'joint' basis. To find out more contact your local authority.

### What other State housing grants might be available to me?

There are various other grants available from the State including:

- *Affordable housing.* Many new developments now include a percentage of what is referred to as 'affordable housing'. These are houses, flats or building sites which must be sold at well below market price to people who would not otherwise be able to afford to buy their own home;
- *Improvement grants.* A range of loans may be available from your local authority in very specific cases so that you can improve or extend your home in certain designated areas;
- *Mortgage subsidy.* If you are a local authority tenant and you give up your home to buy a property on the open market, you may be entitled to financial support for up to five years;
- *Disabled persons grant.* Given to cover the cost of adapting a private home for the needs of someone who is disabled; and
- *Thatching grant.* Available towards the cost of renewing or repairing thatched roofs on houses.

For more information about these grants contact your local authority or the Department of the Environment, Ballina, Co. Mayo on 1890 305030.

### Is it worth repaying my mortgage early?

Should you over-pay your mortgage each month? Should you use all your available cash to reduce your mortgage? Should you use a lump sum of cash to reduce or pay off your mortgage? The answer is *probably* yes if the following applies to you:

- You don't have any other, more expensive, debts. (If you do these should be paid off first);
- It won't leave you without some savings tucked away against a rainy day; and
- There aren't other investment opportunities which might be worth more to you in cash terms.

If you are thinking of paying off some or all of your mortgage I would strongly advise consulting an adviser first. He or she will be able to work out the figures for you.


### What different sorts of home insurance will I need?

This is covered in greater detail in the chapter on insurance. In summary, homeowners should take out the following cover:

- *Building insurance.* This will be compulsory if you have a mortgage. Basically, it means that if some damage is done to the fabric of your home (by a fire or flood, for instance) then money is available to repair or rebuild as necessary;
- *Contents insurance.* This protects you against loss or damage of your home contents and may include 'all risks', e.g. your golf clubs left in the boot of your car; and
- *Mortgage repayment insurance.* This cover means that if you are ill, have an accident or are made redundant, your mortgage repayments would be paid for you. Payments usually last for up to a year after which you are on your own!


### If I have trouble making my mortgage repayments what should I do?

You should immediately contact your lender. The worst thing you can do is keep them in the dark about any financial problems you may be encountering. If you need help with your finances you could contact:

- Your local St Vincent de Paul Society who run a special advice scheme.
- The Department of Social Welfare — who also run a free advice scheme called MABS (Money and Budgeting Advice Services). Details from your local Social Welfare Office or public library.

---

*The Money Doctor says ...*
- Don't be complacent. Even a small difference in the rate you pay can make a huge difference to the cost of your mortgage. No lender deserves your loyalty. Go to where the best deal is.

- Don't trust any adviser who isn't authorised to act for *all* the financial institutions offering home loans in Ireland. There are currently 13 lenders and anyone who can't tell you about *all* of them isn't going to get you the best deal.

- Remember, mortgage advisers are independent and you don't have to pay for their services *plus* they can find you the best package for your needs.

- If in doubt seek expert help, especially when it comes to taking out home loan equity release loans for the over 65s.

# 10

## BETTER BORROWING

### A COMPREHENSIVE GUIDE TO BORROWING, FROM CREDIT CARDS TO CREDIT UNIONS

If there is one area of personal finance where consumers are regularly taken to the cleaners, it is that of personal loans. Banks can charge anything from 6.5% a year (that's €65 for every €1,000 borrowed) to 20% (that's €200 for every €1,000 borrowed) or more *to the same customer*. In the circumstances, it makes sound sense to make sure you are paying as little as possible for your borrowing.

### Sensible borrowing

As already discussed in the chapter on paying off all your debts, there are times when it can make sense to borrow. For instance:

- To buy, build or improve your home;
- To finance a property investment;
- To pay for education;
- To pay for a car or other necessary item; and
- To start a business.

There are also times when it may be impossible not to borrow money; if you are temporarily unable to earn an income, for instance, for some reason beyond your control.

There is no intrinsic harm, either, in genuine short-term borrowing for some luxury item. What is really dangerous, however, is short-term borrowing that becomes long-term borrowing without you meaning it to do so. This is not only extremely expensive but makes you more vulnerable to financial problems. I can't emphasise sufficiently how bad it is for your financial well-being to borrow money to pay for living expenses. In particular, you should definitely avoid long-term credit card and store card debt.

If you have succumbed to the temptation of credit card or store card debt, and you want to pay it off, read the chapter on getting out of debt.

## MONEY DOCTOR WEALTH CHECK

*Never borrow for longer than you have to*
Making sure you pay the lowest rate of interest is one way to keep the cost of borrowing down. Paying your debts back quickly is another. Compound interest really works against you when borrowing money. The difference between paying back €1,000 at 15% APR over one year and, say, three years is a staggering €300 in interest!

## Why rates differ so widely

Financial institutions set their charges according to the level of risk involved and prevailing market conditions.

As far as they are concerned, loans fall into two categories:

*Secured loans* Where, if the borrower fails to make the repayments, there is a physical asset, such as a house or even an insurance policy, that can be seized and sold to meet the outstanding debt. Because of this secured loans should cost considerably less.

*Unsecured loans* Where, if the borrower fails to make the repayments, the lender has no security and thus risks never getting paid (though this is rare). Such loans cost considerably more.

## The first rule of borrowing

The first rule of borrowing for less is, therefore, to take out a secured rather than an unsecured loan. This isn't always practicable, but where it is, you'll save a substantial amount of money.

### *Secured Loans*

Mortgage on your property

Secured loan (second mortgage) on your property

Asset finance (used, for instance, for major purchases such as cars or something that has value and can be resold upon repossession if the loan is defaulted)

### *Unsecured Loans*

Bank overdraft

Credit Union loans

Personal or term loans — including car loans

Credit cards

Store cards

Hire purchase

Money lenders

## Comparing rates

In order that consumers can compare interest rates, the government insists that the cost of loans is expressed in terms of an annual percentage rate, or APR. (See the Jargon Buster for a definition of APR at the back of this book.)

Confusingly, there is more than one way to calculate the APR, but broadly speaking it is an accurate way of assessing how much a loan is going to cost you *including* all the hidden costs such as up-front fees.

Clearly, the lower the APR the cheaper the loan and the better it is for you.

Remember, financial institutions make enormous profits from lending money. You should never, ever be shy about shopping around or asking for a lower rate.

## The Money Doctor Top Loan Guide

Here are the *ten* most usual ways of borrowing money ranked in order — starting with the least expensive and ending with the most expensive.

## *1. Loans from family, friends and employers*

Often family members, friends and employers will make interest-free or low-interest loans. My advice is always to regularise such loans with a written agreement so that there is no room for misunderstanding or bad feeling at a later date.

## 2. Mortgages and secured loans

In the current, low-interest-rate climate, mortgages and secured loans can be amazingly inexpensive. It may be worth your while to add major purchases into your mortgage in order to reduce their real cost. However, bear in mind that if you, say, buy a car and add it to your mortgage, what you should do is increase your monthly repayments so that that bit of your debt is paid off in less time. Otherwise you could be paying for your car over the whole term of your mortgage.

## 3. Asset finance and leasing

I am a big believer in asset finance and leasing — funding assets such as cars, computers, office furniture, telephone systems and electronic equipment over a generally short-term lease period. Although not as cheap as a mortgage this can be an economical way for you to fund major purchases and it has the benefit of being very tax efficient if you are self-employed or running a business. You should ask your adviser to find you the best possible rate.

## 4. Overdrafts

If you have a bank current account you can ask your manager for an overdraft facility. Once approved, you will be able to spend money up to this amount. There won't be a set repayment period BUT there may well be an annual arrangement charge. Authorised overdrafts are usually fairly competitive (though you shouldn't be afraid to negotiate).

Exceeding your overdraft limit, however, can lead to heavy charges and the embarrassment of bounced cheques; for this reason unauthorised overdrafts should be avoided. Bear in mind, too, that most banks expect your current account to be in credit for 30 days a year and will charge you extra if you aren't.

## 5. Credit Union loans

We are fortunate, in Ireland, to have a network of local credit unions willing to lend money to its membership base at a competitive rate of interest. To qualify for a loan you must first join the credit union and then, normally, save a regular amount with them for a set period of time. Because credit unions are non-profit-making they tend to offer much better value for money. Not all credit union rates are the same and it is worth shopping around as your work location may be different to your home location (with credit unions, you MUST live or work locally).

## 6. Personal or term loans

The cost of personal or term loans can vary enormously. Essentially, when you borrow the money you agree to a set repayment period or term. The rate of interest charged is normally variable and you should always pay close attention to your statements to check that it hasn't risen out of line with market rates. Where a rate is fixed in advance, giving you the security of knowing what your repayments will be, it is likely to be higher.

Where a loan is provided by a dealer or retailer, check the conditions closely. Sometimes you could be offered a low or zero rate for an agreed period that will rise dramatically in cost after the set term. Also, the cost of providing this credit will be built into the price of whatever you are buying.

## 7. Credit cards

Used properly a credit card will give you as much as 45 days interest-free credit. On a certain day every month your bill will be calculated for the previous 30 days and sent to you for payment by the end of the following month. If your cut-off date is, say, the seventeenth of the month, all charges between 17 December and 17 January would have to be paid for by the end of February. If you can't pay the full amount then you are given the option of paying a reduced amount. This could be less than 5% of the total outstanding. The catch is that you will be charged an extremely high rate of interest, possibly approaching 20% a year. Credit cards are an extremely expensive way to borrow and credit card companies are very aggressive in their marketing methods. If you are going to use a credit card then don't fall into the trap of making the minimum payment each month. A relatively small balance could take you years to clear.

Note: if your income is high enough your bank may offer you a 'gold' credit card with a built-in overdraft facility at a preferential rate. Your credit card balance will be settled each month using the overdraft. This can be a cost-effective way to borrow and is worth investigating.

## 8. Store cards

I am afraid I am not at all enthusiastic about store cards. They work in the same way as credit cards except, of course, you can only use them in the store (or chain of stores) that issues the card. Their single advantage is that having such a card may entitle you to an extra discount on first purchase and again during any sales. Their huge disadvantage is that the rate of interest charged on outstanding balances almost always makes normal credit cards look cheap by comparison. My strong advice, unless you are very disciplined with money, is only use store cards where there are exceptional discounts and transparent value.

## 9. Hire purchase

Hire purchase allows you to buy specific goods over an agreed period of time. In other words, it is a bit like a personal or term loan. The difference is that the rates charged for hire purchase are normally somewhat higher and you might be better approaching looking at alternatives such as a personal loan or a lease. Remember, too, that with hire purchase you don't own whatever you are buying until you have made your last payment. This is not the case with a personal loan.

## 10. Money lenders

Whether licensed or unlicensed, money lenders are always about the most expensive way to borrow, and the rates they charge are outrageous. When they are trading illegally, there is the added risk of violence or intimidation if you don't pay what they say you owe them. You should avoid them like the plague! Incidentally, the definition of a money lender — and licensed at that — is an entity or someone who charges you a minimum 23% interest per annum! (Check with the Central Bank for a list of licensed money lenders.)

*The Money Doctor says ...*

- Think carefully before you borrow money. Is it sensible to take out a loan for whatever you are planning to buy? Don't borrow money to pay for 'lifestyle' items. No loan should ever last for longer than the thing you are spending the money on!

- Shop around for the most competitive rate. There is a huge difference and you can save yourself, literally, thousands of euro by making sure you have the cheapest possible loan.

- Don't allow your short-term borrowing to become long-term borrowing by mistake.

- Don't be blindly loyal to any particular lender. Go where the best rate is, or the product best suited to your particular needs.

# 11

## PROTECTING YOURSELF AND YOUR FAMILY

### ARRANGING THE BEST MEDICAL, INCOME AND LIFE COVER AT THE LOWEST POSSIBLE PRICE

First class medical protection, critical illness cover and life insurance is available at a remarkably low price providing you know how to buy it.

In this chapter you'll discover:

- How to make sure you aren't sold cover you don't need;
- How to decide what cover it is sensible for you to take out;
- Whom you can trust to advise you; and
- How to make sure you get your cover at the lowest possible price.

Woody Allen, the American film maker, once said that his idea of hell was to be stuck in a lift with a life insurance salesman. Mr Allen is by no means alone in his distrust of both life insurance and the people who sell it. Why should this be? I'm sure it is partly because no one likes to think about anything bad happening to them, and partly because, in order to draw attention to a very real need, life insurance salesmen are forced to bring up uncomfortable subjects with their prospective clients.

However, although it is not something you may rush to

tackle, making certain that you have adequate life and health insurance will bring you *genuine* peace of mind.

## You know you should

It is not pleasant to dwell on being ill, having an accident or, worst of all, dying. Nevertheless, you owe it to yourself, and those you care for, to spend a little time making sure you are *protected* should the worst happen:

*Protected* by PHI (permanent health insurance) if you are too unwell to earn an income;

*Protected* by private medical insurance if you need medical attention; and

*Protected* by life cover if you, or your partner, should die.

For a relatively small amount of money you can take out a range of insurance policies designed to:

- Provide for you, or your dependents, if you or your partner should die.
- Give you a lump sum or a regular income if you find you have a serious illness, are incapacitated or cannot work.
- Meet all your private medical bills in the event of an accident or illness.

There are, of course, plenty of facts and figures available proving just how likely it is for someone of any age to fall ill or die. Sadly, such statistics are borne out by everyone's personal experience. We all know of instances where families have had to face poor medical care and/or financial hardship as the result of a tragedy. We all know, too, that spending the small sum required to purchase appropriate cover makes sound sense.

## Spend time, not money

The odd thing about the different types of insurance dealt with in this chapter is that none of them are expensive when you consider the protection they offer. The secret is to identify exactly what cover you *really* need and not to get sold an inappropriate or over-priced policy. It is also important to review your needs on a regular basis. What you require today, and what you'll require in even two or three years' time, could alter dramatically.

The best way to start is by considering what risks you face and deciding what action you should take. Here are three questions that *everyone* should ask themselves, regardless of their age, gender, health or financial circumstances.

## QUESTION 1: What would your financial position be if you were unable to work, due to an accident or illness, for more than a short period of time?

Obviously your employer and the State will both be obliged to help you out. However, if you have a mortgage, other debts and/or a family to support, your legal entitlements are unlikely to meet anything like your normal monthly outgoings. If you do have a family then your spouse will have to balance work, caring for you and, possibly, caring for children. Is this feasible or, more to the point, desirable? How long will your savings last you under these circumstances? Do you have other assets you could sell?

Unless you have substantial savings and/or low outgoings then *income protection cover* (sometimes known as Permanent Health Insurance) and/or *critical illness insurance* could both make sound sense.

*QUESTION 2: Do you have anyone dependent on you for either financial support or care? Are you dependent on someone else financially? Do you have children — or other family members — who would have to be cared for if you were to die?*

If you are single and don't have any dependents then the reason to take out *life insurance* is in order to settle any debts and/or leave a bequest. If, on the other hand, there is someone depending on you, either for money or for care, then life cover has to be a priority.

If you are supporting anyone (or if your financial contribution is necessary to the running of your household) then you need to take out cover so that you don't leave those you love facing a financial crisis.

If you are caring for anyone, children, perhaps, or an ageing relative, then you should take out cover so that there is plenty of money for someone else to take over this role.

*QUESTION 3: Does it matter to you how quickly you receive non-urgent medical treatment? If you need medical care would you rather choose who looks after you, where you are treated and in what circumstances? How important is a private room in hospital to you?*

We are fortunate enough to enjoy free basic health care in Ireland. However, if you are self-employed or if you have responsibilities which mean that it is important for you to be able to choose the time and place of any medical treatment, then you should consider *private medical insurance* such as VHI or BUPA.

## Income protection cover

If you are of working age then the chances of you being off work for a prolonged period of time due to illness or an accident are substantially greater than the chances of you dying. It is for this reason that income protection cover or Permanent Health Insurance is so valuable. As its name suggests, it is designed to replace up to 66% of your income if a disability or serious illness prevents you from working.

*It is the only form of assurance outside pension life cover that offers tax relief at your marginal rate on the premiums paid.*

If you are in a company pension scheme or if you have arranged your own pension you should check to see what cover you have already since it is sometimes included.

Incidentally, most policies only pay out after the policyholder has been off work for a minimum of thirteen weeks *unless* hospitalised. Also, if you want to reduce the cost you can opt for a policy that doesn't pay out until you have been off work for 26 weeks.

---

*The Money Doctor says ...*
As with anything *you should shop around* for all your insurance cover. Costs vary dramatically. Remember, too, that an authorised professional adviser (Authorised Advisor) can explain all the policies to you and can steer you to the best for your needs.

## MONEY DOCTOR WEALTH WARNING

*Don't be sold something you don't need*

I don't believe it is advisable to buy insurance from anyone who isn't qualified to inform you about every single option available to you. Salesmen who are tied to one company, or even a small selection of companies, are clearly not going to offer you the same quality of advice as someone who has a detailed knowledge of the entire market. For further advice on this crucial area see Chapter 7.

## Critical or serious illness insurance

Horrible as it is to think about, imagine being diagnosed with a serious illness. I am talking about something like cancer, heart disease or multiple sclerosis. Naturally, under the circumstances, you might need special care and/or want to make life changes. This is where critical or serious illness insurance comes in. Providing you survive for two weeks after your diagnosis, you will receive a lump sum of tax-free money to spend however you wish. Clearly such a sum would allow you to pay off your debts, seek specialist treatment or in some other way ensure that you didn't have any financial problems.

It is important to remember that this cover provides you with a lump sum — not an income.

## Life cover

There are several different types of life cover but they are all designed to do one thing. For a relatively low monthly payment they provide a lump sum if the person insured dies. The lump sum is tax-free and may go into the insured's estate or may be directly payable to a nominated person (such as his or her spouse). Some of the uses to which this lump sum might be put include:

- Paying off a mortgage;
- Paying off other debts;
- Being invested to provide a replacement income; and
- Being invested to provide money for childcare or the care of someone else such as an ageing relative.

In the case of more expensive life cover the policy can have a cash-in value after a period of time has elapsed. The cost of life cover will be determined by your age, gender, and lifestyle. If you are a non-smoker and don't drink heavily you will save quite a bit of money.

Below are details of the different types of cover available so that you can decide which is most appropriate to your requirements.

## Term insurance

As its name implies, term insurance is available for a pre-agreed period of time, usually a minimum of 5 years. It is mandatory when you take out interest-only home loans, except if you are over 50 years of age and you choose to waive this cover.

It is particularly useful for people with a temporary need. For instance, if you have young children you and your spouse might take out a 20-year plan giving you protection until your family have grown up and left home. By the same token, you might take out a policy that would pay off the exact amount of your mortgage.

Term insurance is the least expensive form of life cover and you can opt for:

- *Level Term.* The amount of cover remains the same (level) for the agreed period. For instance, you might take out €50,000 of cover for ten years. The cost will remain fixed for the same period, too.

- *Decreasing Term.* Some people refer to this as mortgage protection. The amount of cover drops (decreases) every year. For instance, you might take out €50,000 of cover that drops to €48,000 in the second year, €45,000 in the third year and so forth. Such policies are almost always taken out in conjunction with mortgages in order to pay off the outstanding debt should the insured die. *Note that this sort of cover can't be extended or increased in value once you have taken it out.*

- *Convertible Term.* Although the cover is for a set period of time a convertible policy will allow you to extend your insurance for a further period regardless of your health. This is a very useful feature because it means that if you suffer some health problem you won't be denied life cover because of it. In fact, if you extend the policy the insurance company will charge you the same premium as if you were perfectly healthy. Convertible term cover is normally not much more expensive than level term cover and is therefore usually the better option.

## Whole-of-life assurance

There are two benefits to taking out a 'whole-of-life' assurance plan. Firstly, providing you carry on making your monthly payments, the plan is guaranteed to pay out. In other words, you are covered for the whole of your life.

Secondly, there can be an investment element to the cover. So if you decide to cancel the plan you'll receive back a lump sum.

There are various features you can opt for with whole-of-life cover. You can vary the balance between actual life cover and the investment element, for instance. Also you can decide to end the cover at a particular point, when you retire for instance. Some whole-of-life policies are designed to meet inheritance tax liabilities.

Whole-of-life cover is obviously more expensive than term or decreasing cover.

## Private medical insurance

This type of insurance is designed to meet some or all of your medical bills if you opt to go for private treatment.

Only two companies currently provide this cover in Ireland. VHI (Voluntary Health Insurance) and BUPA. Between them they offer a wide range of plans with an array of options, conditions and limits.

The basic decisions you have to make are:

- Do you want a choice of consultant?
- Do you want a choice of hospital?
- Do you want private or just semi-private hospital accommodation? and
- Do you want outpatient cover?

Discounts can be available if you join through a group, your employer, for instance, or a credit union.

As with all insurance it is well worth getting expert help in deciding which option is best for your needs.

## Which types of cover should you choose?

Is it better to take out income protection or critical illness insurance? Should you opt for term life or whole-of-life cover? If term cover, which sort? If whole-of-life, what investment element should you include? Do you need private medical insurance, or is it a luxury you can do without?

Although these are personal decisions that only you can make, *a professional Authorised Advisor will be able to guide you.* You can trust these advisers to give you the best possible advice because they are bound by law to do so, and can be prosecuted for mis-selling.

The following comments may also help you:

- If you have a limited budget I would opt, first and foremost, for either income protection or critical illness cover. Depending on your circumstances you might take out both.
- If you are on a tight budget then take out decreasing term insurance to cover your mortgage.
- If you have joint financial responsibilities, for instance, if you are married, and you have limited resources, it is more important to cover the main income earner.
- Covering a husband and wife together on the same policy often doesn't cost that much more than covering just one person.
- If you are self-employed, private medical cover is not really a luxury but more of a necessity and the premiums are tax deductible for everyone.

## Keeping the cost down

There are two ways to keep the cost of your insurance down to an absolute minimum.

To begin with, of course, you should always get independent professional assistance from someone who is authorised to look at *every conceivable option* for you. This is one purchase where shopping around and expert knowledge can save you serious money.

Secondly, *refine your needs*. By taking out the *right sort* of cover and the *right level* of cover you won't be wasting money.

---

*The Money Doctor says ...*

- Don't stick your head in the sand, believing that 'it won't happen to me'. Protecting yourself and your family should be one of your key financial priorities.

- Choose an independent, professional *authorised* adviser who you feel comfortable with to advise you.

- Don't get sold cover you don't need.

- Review your needs regularly — every two or three years — to make sure you have adequate protection.

- This is a fiercely competitive market. Having an expert shop around for you could mean big savings.

---

# 12

## PROTECTING YOUR POSSESSIONS & OTHER ASSETS

### INSIDE TIPS ON KEEPING THE COST OF YOUR GENERAL INSURANCE TO A BARE MINIMUM

With the cost of general insurance only going one way, it is important to make sure that you are getting value for money. In this chapter you'll discover:

- Details of all the different types of cover you should consider;
- How to ensure that you aren't paying more than you have to; and
- Other buying tips.

### The importance of proper cover

The temptation, when insurance premiums rise, is to reduce the amount of cover you have or, where cover isn't obligatory, to cancel the policy completely.

There are two reasons why it is important to make sure that you have adequate general insurance.

Firstly, if you have borrowed money in order to pay for something you should always ensure that there is sufficient insurance to repay the debt in case disaster strikes. To quote just one case history:

Frank borrowed €15,000 to buy a car and only took out

the cheapest motor insurance he could buy — third-party, fire and theft. The car was involved in an accident and completely destroyed. Because Frank didn't have comprehensive insurance he is now saddled with paying off the original car loan plus paying for a replacement car.

Secondly, if you *under*-insure then you always risk receiving less of a pay-out when you come to claim. This is particularly true when it comes to home insurance. Again, let me quote a real case history:

John and Moira didn't have a mortgage on their house and, although they had buildings and contents protection, they hadn't bothered to check the amount of cover for many years. Unfortunately an electrical fault resulted in the house being burned down (thankfully, no one was hurt). When they came to claim, because they were under-insured, the insurance company would only pay three-quarters of the price of rebuilding. This is known as the 'average clause' — *caveat emptor!*

Shopping around for insurance is no one's idea of fun. On the other hand, the cost of not taking out adequate insurance can be huge. And if you invest even a small amount of time reading this chapter and acting on it you will keep the cost to a bare minimum.

## The different types of 'general' insurance

So what is general insurance anyway? It is a catch-all expression encompassing some of the following areas:

- Home and other forms of property insurance.
- Motor insurance.
- Public liability.

- Insurance for your other possessions such as boats, caravans and mobile telephones.
- Pet insurance.
- Travel insurance.
- Specialist risks — golf cover (having to buy a round of drinks after a hole in one!).
- Credit insurance.
- Professional indemnity insurance.

## *Don't just rely on general insurance brokers*

General insurance is the one area where I would suggest that you shouldn't rely solely on brokers to get you the best deal. In many areas there are now 'direct' operations that can substantially undercut brokers. To find details of these direct operations look in the *Golden Pages* and keep an eye out for companies advertising in the national press. Remember, too, that some insurance companies tend to rely on customer inertia when it comes to renewal. So, having won your custom, they may push the cost of cover up in the second year hoping that you won't be bothered to check elsewhere. Telephoning around and filling in extra paperwork is a nuisance but think of it this way: if it takes you, say, three hours work to save €200, then you are effectively paying yourself nearly €70 an hour after tax.

## Home insurance

Home insurance is divided into buildings cover and contents cover.

*Buildings cover* is obligatory if you have a mortgage and you may find that your lender automatically provides this protection (or, at the very least, a quotation) for you. The insurance will protect the structure of your home (the building itself, outbuildings, fixtures and fittings and so forth) against fire, storm damage, flood, subsidence, and other similar accidents. Most policies also include public liability cover so that if something happens to someone on your property (for instance, if they have an accident) you are protected.

The main thing to watch for with buildings cover is that you have sufficient protection. The cost is worked out on the value of your home and is linked entirely to the rebuilding cost. So where your home is located, how old it is, its size and the materials from which it is constructed, will all influence the premium.

If you would like help deciding how much cover to take out, then the Society of Chartered Surveyors (5 Wilton Place, Dublin 2) produces an annual guide. Not all buildings policies will cover you for the same things so you should check the small print. One way of keeping the cost down is to make sure you have burglar and smoke alarms fitted, while another is to join your local neighbourhood-watch scheme.

*Contents cover* is even less standard than buildings cover. The sort of protection you'll receive can vary enormously and when comparing prices you need to bear this in mind. For instance, are you being offered 'new for old' cover, which means that if you claim you'll receive the exact cost of replacement with no reduction on account of the age of your possessions? Also, how much of the loss will you be expected to pay for yourself (known as the 'excess clause')?

And to what extent are valuables, such as jewellery or cash, actually covered? You'll find that there are all sorts of 'extras' that may or may not be included, from employer's liability to theft of bicycles and from liability to third parties to personal liability. Tedious as it is, the only way to know what you are actually getting is to read the small print. Happily, there are a number of ways in which you can keep the cost of your contents cover down:

- Fit an approved alarm system;
- Fit approved locks to doors and windows;
- Fit smoke alarms; and
- Join your neighbourhood watch scheme.

It is to be noted that discounts are sometimes offered to people at home most of the day, such as those who are retired.

## Buying motor insurance

With such high insurance premiums the temptation is to try and reduce the cost by any means possible. For instance, city-based car owners usually pay higher premiums than their rural counterparts and some are tempted to pretend that their car actually 'lives' in the country. Remember, that if you ever come to claim, many insurance companies now send out an investigator to make independent inquiries and a false statement could result in being taken to court for fraud.

Motor insurance is more expensive if you:

- Don't have a full licence.
- Have a history of motor offences.
- Are under 25 years old.
- Have made claims in the past.
- Have a criminal record.

Obviously you can't make yourself any older than you actually are but if you don't have a full licence it is well worth putting in the effort to pass the test. By the same token, don't rush to put in a minor claim as it may result in higher premiums. Also remember that fines may not be the only cost of speeding.

## Insider tips on buying other general insurance

In my opinion many types of general insurance do not offer value for money. I am particularly suspicious of:

- *Extended warranties.* These cover you against faults developing in your electrical and mechanical goods. Often the retailer makes more money from these insurance policies (by way of commission) than on the sale of the actual product. As legislation offers you 12 months protection anyway (and as, in general, such goods are much better made nowadays) I am suspicious of such policies.

- *Mobile telephone insurance.* Protects you against loss of or damage to your phone. This is often expensive in relation to the actual cost of replacing your telephone. Furthermore, many people end up buying this cover without meaning to because they don't pay proper attention when completing the contract.

- *Credit card insurance.* There are two types of cover offered by credit card companies. The first protects you against fraud and the second against you being unable to make your repayments due to an accident, illness or redundancy. Both types of cover are expensive and in most cases I would advise against them.

- *Pet insurance.* This protects you against having to pay vet bills if your pet is ill or involved in an accident. Again, I would strongly suggest examining the value for money offered by such policies.

One more point in relation to buying *travel insurance*. This is often sold by travel agents at highly inflated prices since they earn good rates of commission on every policy sold. Travel insurance is important, but there are many different sources of cover. If you are a regular traveller you may like to consider an annual policy. Also, if you have a Gold or Platinum credit card a certain amount of cover *may* be included with your annual fee.

---

*The Money Doctor says ...*

- Check the small print! All insurance policies are not equal.

- It may not be much fun shopping around but it helps if you think of the saving in terms of effort and reward. Three hours spent saving €200 is worth virtually €70 an hour after tax to you.

- Don't get sucked in to buying cover you don't really need.

- Don't be tempted to under-insure ... it could leave you exposed.

# *13*

## RETIRE EARLY ... RETIRE RICH

### WITH A SMALL AMOUNT OF PLANNING AND THE BENEFIT OF SOME HUGE TAX BREAKS, IT IS POSSIBLE TO MAKE ALL YOUR RETIREMENT DREAMS COME TRUE

An alternative title for this chapter would be 'pensions made easy' — because it will tell you everything you need to know to:

- Decide what sort of pension you will need;
- Assess your current pension prospects;
- Understand all the various options open to you;
- Arrange a pension that will ensure a comfortable retirement for you;
- Retire early; and
- Find someone you can trust to steer you through the pensions minefield.

It must be emphasised that no one should be complacent about retirement planning. Even if you have a pension you must review it on a regular basis. You could be a long time retired, anything from twenty to forty years, so you need to get it right.

## Why you should make this your number one priority

The only people who don't have to worry about retirement planning are those lucky enough to belong to a really first-class pension scheme (one with generous, cast-iron benefits), or, who are so rich that money will never be a problem.

For the rest of us pension planning should be a top priority — more of a priority, in fact, than almost any other financial decision we take. Frankly, it doesn't matter if you haven't bought your own home or invested a single penny of your money *providing you have a good pension plan.* I say this because, thanks to longer life expectancy, many people will spend anything from twenty to forty years in retirement. In other words, you work for 40 years to retire for 30 years.

Typically, as we get older and progress in our careers we earn more money. However, on retirement we are no longer able to earn an income and must rely on either our savings or State benefits. Our earnings are therefore usually at their highest just before we retire. And unless we have made proper provision they will be at their lowest just after we retire. This can result in a massive drop in lifestyle at the point of retirement.

This is where the concept of Income Equalisation comes in — that is, reducing your disposable income when you are earning good money, to help increase your income when you are not able to earn. We reduce our disposable income now by putting money into a pension scheme that can be used to increase our retirement income. It is still likely that when we retire our income will fall, but with this type of planning the transition will be far less of a shock to the system.

## INCOME DISTRIBUTION THROUGHOUT LIFE — NO PENSION PLANNING

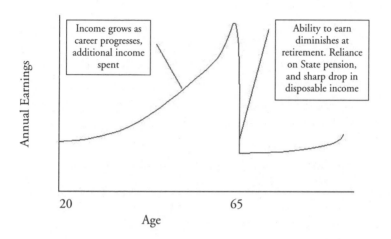

## INCOME EQUALISATION — THROUGH PENSION PLANNING

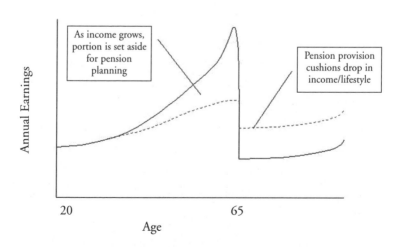

**MONEY DOCTOR WEALTH WARNING**

*Is your company or government pension going to let you down?*

Are you in a company or government pension scheme — outside the State pension which you would be entitled to at age 66 ? You should check on a regular basis, certainly every other year, that it is actually going to meet your needs on retirement. A growing number of pension schemes are producing disappointing returns and you should not be complacent. *Very few company schemes provide enough money to ensure a comfortable old age income.* Get expert help too, because whereas companies are obliged to give you details of your benefits (and losses), you might not necessarily understand them. You can't rely on whoever is operating the scheme to provide you with the information you need.

## It is never too early or late to begin

Given that it is not impossible that your retirement may turn out to be a longer period than that of your working life, it isn't surprising that pension experts stress the importance of starting to plan early.

Nevertheless, if the number of men and women in their forties, fifties and even their sixties consulting the Money Doctor on pension planning is anything to go by, a huge percentage of the population don't start thinking about their retirement until it isn't that far away.

Obviously, the later you leave it the more of your income you will have to devote to building up a decent pension fund and the less well off you can expect to be once you stop work. But just because it is never too late to begin, it doesn't mean you should go to the wire. Every single day counts.

## Start by taking stock of where you are

The first step towards a comfortable retirement is to take stock of where you are now in pension terms:

- Are you part of one or more company or occupational pension schemes already?
- Are you entitled to a State pension by virtue of your employment?
- Are you entitled to non-contributory old age pension?
- Could you live on a quarter of the average industrial wage — because that is roughly what the State pension will give you! and
- Have you started a pension plan in the past?

If you answer 'yes' to any of these questions then you need to find out what your existing pension is going to be worth to you.

You also need to consider what other assets you have. Will your home be paid for by the time you retire? Have you any other savings or investments? By the same token, are there any other debts that you will need to discharge before retirement?

Where do you go for the answers to all these questions ?

The easiest thing to do is to get a qualified professional to do the work for you, in other words either an accountant (if they specialise in this area) or an Authorised Advisor. The alternative is to approach all the relevant parties yourself. That is to say:

- Your current employer;
- Any past employers;
- The managers of any pension scheme you may have started in the past;
- The Department of Community, Family and Social Affairs (check your telephone directory for the relevant department); and
- The Pensions Board, Verschoyle House, Mount Street, Dublin, 2.

If you are unhappy with any aspect of the way a non-government pension scheme has been administered, then you should contact the Pensions Ombudsman, 36 Upper Mount Street, Dublin 2.

> *The Money Doctor says ...*
> If you are *self-employed or you are not in an employer-sponsored pension scheme* then, unless you take action, you'll have to rely on the State. You can guess how well off that will leave you.

## What will you need?

The whole concept of retirement has been turned on its head in recent years. As a population we are:

- Giving up work sooner — often in our late forties or fifties;
- Living longer and healthier lives; and

- Leading more active lives in retirement.

We also expect a much higher standard of living. As a result we need more money in retirement than our predecessors. Here are some things you will need to consider:

- Will you need a lump sum on retirement, to pay off debts or to invest for a regular income?
- Will you still have unavoidable expenses, such as children's education, to pay for?
- How much of an income will you need? Could you manage on half of what you earn now? Could you manage on a quarter?
- What changes would you have to make to your lifestyle if the only money you had coming in after retirement was the State pension? and
- Do you have anyone else to provide for? Your spouse, for instance? What will happen if you die before they do?

Our civil servants receive an index-linked income of up to two-thirds of their final pay, a tax-free sum of up to one-and-a-half year's salary, and a half-pension for their spouses after they die. Only a very tiny percentage of private sector schemes offer this type of benefit.

What's more, if you work in the private sector and wanted to receive the same sort of benefit from the age of 65 *you would have to put about 15% of your income into a pension fund from the age of 20.*

## The good news

There are three excellent reasons why you shouldn't despair, regardless of whether or not you have any sort of pension in place already:

- The government realises that it is vital to encourage you to save for your retirement so they will give you HUGE tax incentives to do so;
- Good planning *at any age* can optimise your retirement income; and
- By taking action now you can dramatically alter your position. It is only people who continue to ignore the risks they are running who face the risk (one might say certainty) of an impoverished retirement.

## What to do if you work in the private sector

If you work for someone else you will be in one of two situations:

Either you will be in a company or occupational scheme

*or*

You won't be in any scheme at all.

If you are in a company or occupational pension scheme then you will need to ascertain how good the scheme is, the sort of pension you can expect, what other benefits you may be entitled to and whether it is possible to increase your pension by making additional voluntary contributions (AVCs). If, on taking expert advice, the existing pension scheme doesn't appear to be that good, then concentrate on those AVCs.

Don't forget any schemes you may have been in during your previous employment.

If you aren't in your employer's scheme (and all employers are now obliged to operate a scheme under recent legislation — Personal Retirement Savings Accounts or PRSAs — or at least have a direct debit provision from your salary to such an investment) then you should consider joining. If you have no pension arrangements at all (and you don't want to do something through your employer) then you need to start a scheme of your own.

Your own pension scheme might be a personal pension plan or the more recently introduced PRSAs. We'll be looking at these options in greater detail in a moment.

## What to do if you work for yourself

If you work for yourself you are going to have to provide your own pension. The big advantage to this is that you can design a pension plan that perfectly matches your needs:

- It will be flexible, allowing you to invest on a regular basis or with lump sums;
- You'll have the choice of investing your money in an established fund or starting your own if you are a company owner, proprietary director (i.e. have at least a 5% shareholding in your company) or a senior company employee, (e.g. a Small Self-Administered Pension Scheme — SSAPs) or Self-Directed Trusts; and
- If you own your own company you could even consider setting up a company scheme.

## A quick guide to pension schemes

One of my teenage daughter's favourite expressions is 'too much information'. It is an emotion frequently expressed by individuals trying to understand the pension system. Nor is it any wonder when you consider how complicated the various options are. Opening a book on the subject at random, a book aimed at ordinary consumers, by the way, my eyes fell immediately on the following sentence:

> 'Where a 5% Director chooses the New Retirement Options they must first ensure that the total fund accumulated would not result in a situation where the maximum benefits would be excluded had they gone down the traditional annuity purchase route.'

My own view is that you should inform yourself, in the same way that you would inform yourself before making any major purchase, but that unless you find the topic fascinating don't waste your time grappling with the minutiae. Instead, let an *independent* and authorised expert advise you. Here, then, is my quick guide to pension schemes.

## Back to basics

Basically a pension scheme, or a retirement plan, or whatever you want to call it, is a way of saving money specifically for your retirement. What differentiates it from an ordinary savings plan is that you will receive substantial help from the taxman and, in exchange, access to your savings will be restricted. How restricted? Well, it will vary but typically you won't be able to touch any of the money you have saved until you reach a minimum age (this will vary according to the scheme and even the sort of job you have) and even then you won't be able to get your hands on all of it as a tax-free lump sum.

## The choices available to you

There are three basic employment categories and the pension options can be defined as follows:

## 1. Employee

• *Occupational pension schemes* — money invested in these schemes is locked away until you actually retire. At that point there will be restrictions on how you take the benefit. For instance, you'll only be allowed a limited amount as a lump sum — tax free — and the rest will have to be taken as an income.

  – *Defined Benefit.* This is the Rolls Royce of schemes and extremely valuable. It can be either a contributory or non-contributory scheme — invariably the employer will make contributions to the scheme. With this type of pension the employer guarantees you a certain percentage of your final salary, as a pension for life, for every year you have been working for them. Depending on the particular scheme this can be up to 66% of the annual average of your last three years' income. You can also elect to take part of your benefits as a tax-free lump sum of up to one-and-a-half times your salary. The beauty of defined benefit schemes is that, irrespective of fund performance, you are guaranteed to receive the promised pension. It is the trustees of the scheme who have to worry about how they are going to fund what could be a very expensive company cost. More and more employers are opting out of the defined benefit pension because of cost, a trend exacerbated by the poor pension fund performances of the late Nineties and first part of the new century.

  Defined benefit schemes undoubtedly provide the best pension benefits. However, you should note that benefits are based on how long you have been working for that company. If you have a relatively short number of years service you can still top up your pension benefits by making some extra contributions through Additional Voluntary Contributions (see below).

- *Defined Contribution.* Your pension is based on the growth of your monthly contributions (again the employer will usually also make contributions to your pension) up to maturity on retirement age. Unfortunately, there is no guarantee of how much you will receive on retirement as values may fall as well as rise. Your fund is purely down to how fund managers perform and how much you have invested. It is vital therefore that you are fully briefed and communicated with on a regular basis so that you can take corrective action if necessary. That corrective action may be an AVC.

- *Additional Voluntary Contributions (AVCs).* Depending on your own existing pension contribution and your age, you could put up to 30% of your annual income into an AVC. You can offset the entire 30% against your income tax liability, making this procedure a very tax efficient one.

Furthermore, most employers will deduct your AVCs directly from your wages. If they do this you will also benefit from PRSI relief on your AVC. There is also greater flexibility about how and when you take the benefits and you won't have to pay for setting up a scheme of your own.

If your employer's pension scheme has a good investment performance or guaranteed benefits, then putting more money into it via an AVC can make excellent financial sense.

Check with an Authorised Advisor for specific details, as there are so many regulations and you want to ensure you're making the right decision.

- *No occupational pension scheme available to you.* If your employer does not offer an occupational pension scheme you have the same options as someone who is self-employed (see below). The one exception is that your employer is required, by law, to provide you with a pay-roll deduction facility to a nominated PRSA provider.

## 2. Self-Employed

- *PRSA/Personal Pensions* — with the recent introduction of PRSAs, pensions became more accessible and less expensive to start. PRSAs have maximum charges of 5% of each premium paid plus 1%, a year, of the accumulated fund. *The affordable pension is here to stay:*

  - Low cost;
  - Generous tax relief at your marginal rate. Depending on your age this can be on contributions of up to 30% of your income;
  - Easy to understand — you decide how much you want to invest and where you want the money invested;
  - Flexible in that you can bring the pension with you from employment to employment together with flexibility in being able to adjust your annual contributions depending on your circumstances, and flexible about how you use the fund on retirement;
  - When you retire, you can have up to 25% of the fund as a tax-free lump sum (useful for paying off a mortgage); and

— Suitable for people who work for themselves, have no company scheme or change their employment frequently.

In theory, a PRSA is a simplified version of a personal pension plan. In practice, the rules governing PRSAs are just as complicated. You should seek independent advice.

## 3. Directors

• *Directors' executive pensions (for those with a 5% or more shareholding in their company)*
The advantages offered by company schemes are so good that if you are self-employed (a sole trader), it may even be worth your while to form a limited company in order to avail of them. If you do own your own company, then setting up a company pension scheme will probably be the best route for you. The main reason for this is that the limits for which the Revenue will give tax relief on pension contributions are significantly higher for a company investing in a company pension scheme than for an individual investing in a corresponding PRSA or personal pension.

Company schemes can be arranged to benefit as many employees as you want, just you, or selected members of your staff, as you prefer. Note that this route is particularly good for anyone who has left it late in life to plan for their retirement.

— As there is no benefit-in-kind on contributions to a company pension scheme, your company will be able to put substantial tax-free money into your pension;

— There is greater flexibility with regard to your retirement date;

- You have more control over where your contributions are invested; and

- You can take a portion of your fund tax-free — so *tax breaks on the way in and the way out!*

• *PRSAs/Personal Pensions* (see number 2. above)
• *Small Self Administered Pension Schemes (SSAP) or Self-Directed Trusts*

Under most pension arrangements it is left up to fund managers to determine what the pension funds actually invest in. However, if you want more direct control on the actual assets that make up your pension fund you can always set up a SSAP. Here you appoint a Pensioneer Trustee to run your pension but you dictate what it invests in. For example, if you want to invest in shares you can pick the individual shares as opposed to just which managed fund.

Recent legislative changes have also brought in for the first time a provision which allows pension funds to borrow for property acquisition. This effectively means that you could borrow within your pension fund to buy an investment property (at arm's length — not your own company's offices, your holiday hot spot or your granny's flat) and both the rental income contributions and your own monthly contributions will be paid into your pension fund tax-free, while all along your fund (i.e. your property) should be appreciating as you are making those contributions. There is also the added benefits that no capital gains liability is incurred and your estate keeps the asset (i.e. your property) after you die.

I think that for the company executive the SSAPs/Self-Directed Trusts will grow considerably over the coming

years as a result of the introduction of that one
provision: allowing pension funds to borrow or gear
perhaps up to four times the fund value to buy
investment property.

SSAPs are not just confined to property. Shares,
investments and even complex financial instruments (e.g.
hedge funds) can be incorporated into SSAPs.

## BIG tax relief — the Revenue Commissioners are on your side

I have made repeated mention of the huge tax incentives
offered to those who invest in a pension. These include:

- Tax relief at your marginal rate of tax. So if you are paying
  tax at 42% *when you put €100 into your pension fund it
  will only cost you €58.* Put another way, pension funds
  almost double the value of your savings before the money
  has been invested in anything;
- Investments grow tax-free;
- If you put money into your own company scheme it is a
  legitimate business expense for tax purposes;
- It can be possible to save PRSI when you put money into
  a pension for either you or your company, depending on
  what type of pension you take out;
- While it is in a pension fund, no income tax or Capital
  Gains Tax (CGT) is payable on your investment; and
- All pension schemes allow you to take out a certain
  portion of your fund tax-free when you come to retire.

There are limits on the amount you can invest into a pension
and still get the tax relief.

## What happens to your pension contributions?

If you are part of an occupational pension scheme then your money will be invested by the scheme's managers. If it is a big scheme they may invest it directly themselves. Most companies, however, use the services of professional fund managers who invest in everything from stocks and shares to property and commodities. Performance will be determined by how well the scheme is managed and if you are in a 'defined contribution' scheme you need to pay close attention to this. For employer-sponsored schemes (e.g occupational pension schemes) *trustees* play an important role as they look after the investment decisions on advice from fund managers.

If you set up your own personal pension plan or your own company sets up a company scheme, then you have much more control over how your contributions are invested while *you* have to make the investment choices. Most opt for *equity funds* — where your money is pooled and invested in stocks and shares. Such funds will have varying returns and different levels of risk. As you near retirement you will be less likely to place your fund in a higher risk investment than you would if you were in your early 30s.

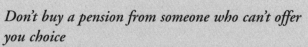

**MONEY DOCTOR WEALTH WARNING**

*Don't buy a pension from someone who can't offer you choice*
All the financial institutions involved in the retirement market, and I'm speaking chiefly about life insurance companies and banks, employ

salesmen whose job it is to promote their own company's pension plans.

One such example is that of a young female solicitor who was persuaded to take out a bancassurance pension plan at a premium of more than €500 per month, based on her expectation of a certain income on retirement in keeping with her current levels of salary. After a couple of months she cancelled the policy because she was not asked one of the most important questions '*Can you afford to pay this amount each month into a pension scheme?*'

While it is important to aim for a similar level of income to retire on, it is equally important to be able to afford it and have a life in the meantime.

Ideally you should not choose a pension from someone who only represents one company.

You should always deal with someone independent who is *authorised* to tell you about *every single option available to you*. Pension fund performance and management fees vary enormously. Buying without comparing the whole market could cost you a great deal of money.

## What is it going to cost?

Almost without exception the pension industry gets paid on commission. This commission comes out of your monthly payments. The amount will vary according to the type of pension scheme you join or set up. Many schemes (but not all) will involve an initial, one-off fee followed by an annual management charge. To give you an example, for a standard PRSA the maximum annual management charge is 1% of the accumulated fund, whilst the initial set-up fee is capped at 5% of the premiums. When you take out a pension your Authorised Advisor will explain, in full, what charges you are paying. *Remember, however, the charges are one thing, but what is it going to cost to provide an income?*

Having a pension is one thing, but having a pension which is going to provide you with the income you think you will need is another. One example of this was a shop-owner who sought advice on investing a lump sum. One suggestion was to look at investing this in a pension. However, he indicated that he was alright here as he had already put a pension in place. It transpired that this 45-year-old shop-owner was currently earning €50,000 a year and had just taken out a pension plan for €400 a month. He was shocked to learn that if he kept contributions at this level, and took the State contributory pension into account, he could expect to have a total after-tax retirement income of around €750 a month (in today's terms) at age 65 — a fraction of what he currently earned.

You get what you pay for. One way of looking at it is to look at what level of income you think you need and seeing how much it would cost to provide this. You may not be able to afford the cost now but at least you will know what to expect.

Below is a table which shows the approximate costs of funding a total after-tax income of €1,250 a month and €2,500 a month in today's terms should you retire at 65. They assume that you will be entitled to the State Contributory Pension. These figures are meant as a guide only and make a number of assumptions. You should discuss your own particular circumstances with a qualified Authorised Adviser.

| | Aged 25 | Aged 30 | Aged 35 | Aged 40 | Aged 45 | Aged 50 | Aged 55 |
|---|---|---|---|---|---|---|---|
| €1,250pm | €191pm | €255pm | €347pm | €482pm | €673pm | €1,001pm | €1,681pm |
| €2,500pm | €341pm | €457pm | €623pm | €864pm | €1,207pm | €1,79 pm | €3,019pm |

*The above figures are before tax relief, and assume that contributions are increased by 5% a year, inflation is 5% a year and the State pension increases by 5% a year. It also assumes that the funds the pension is invested in increase by 6% a year and that tax rates on retirement are similar to today.

## What benefits should you be looking for?

How do you judge a pension scheme? Here are some tips:

- If it is a *defined benefit* scheme then you should judge it primarily on what percentage of your salary you'll receive once you retire. Remember, these are the only schemes where the benefit is guaranteed based on service and salary.
- Depending on the type of pension plan you have you will be given a certain portion, by way of a tax-free lump sum, of the fund's value. Establish how much.
- Death-in-service benefit. Essentially this is life cover giving your beneficiaries a lump sum and/or an income should you die before retirement age.
- Death-in-retirement benefit. This gives your beneficiaries a lump sum and/or an income if you die after you have retired.
- The minimum retirement age (for occupational pension schemes it is 60, but if you own your company you can take a well-earned rest at age 50).
- How much your pension income will increase each year after you have started claiming it. Will it increase in line with the cost of living? More than the cost of living?

- Any special benefits offered to your spouse or other dependents.

## What happens when you retire?

This will depend on your employment status and scheme.

For *defined benefit schemes*, you will receive a tax-free lump sum and a guaranteed annual income, usually index-linked and based on your service.

For *defined contribution schemes*, the accumulated fund on retirement is used to buy annuity income based on how much is in the fund after taking out an allowable portion by way of a tax-free lump sum.

For funds accumulated through *director schemes, AVCs, PRSAs or personal pensions*, the choices are greater as recent legislation brought in new options — *Approved Retirement Funds (ARFs)* and *Approved Minimum Retirement Funds (AMRFs)* — allowing pension funds to be held outside of annuities (see Jargon Buster for a definition) and effectively kept within your estate when you pass on. The taxable benefits can be taken as needed. If you have an annuity, the insurance company keeps the money when you die and your dependents lose out.

---

*The Money Doctor says ...*
- You are probably, to quote a line from the television series *Black Adder*, perfectly happy to wear cotton without understanding how the weaving process works. By the same token, you shouldn't feel that you need to understand

---

pensions legislation in its entirety to make your retirement plans!

- Action is imperative. If you have a really good pension plan, allowing you to retire early, you don't need any other investments (not even a house).

- The sooner you act the better it will be *but* it is never too late to start. Extra tax benefits may apply the older you are.

- The tax benefits are ENORMOUS. For a tax payer on the higher rate of tax, €100 into a pension will currently only cost €58. This is a bargain by anyone's standards. Also, if it incorporates life cover you may receive extra tax relief.

- Please, please take independent professional advice. I am repeating myself, I know. But only someone who is authorised to advise you on every pension available is going to guarantee you the most appropriate pension for your needs.

# 14

## CREATING YOUR OWN SAFETY NET

### THE QUICKEST, MOST EFFICIENT WAY TO BUILD UP AN EMERGENCY FUND

One of your key financial objectives should be to have some easily accessible cash savings to pay for larger expenses or simply in case of a rainy day. In this chapter you will discover:

- Why it is so important to have cash savings;
- How much savings you should build up; and
- The best way to make your savings grow.

### Good, old-fashioned savings

We are lucky enough to live in a country where the State will provide a safety net for widows, those who are seriously ill or disabled, pensioners and others in dire financial straits. However, the amount on offer is relatively meagre and won't cover most of the day-to-day financial crises ordinary people face. For instance, the State isn't going to help you with an unexpected bill for repairs to your home or car. Nor will they pay all your regular bills if you find yourself without an income for any reason whatsoever. The fact is you should have a bit of cash tucked away — good, old fashioned savings — just in case you ever need it. You should probably also have some extra cash to hand:

- to take advantage of an unexpected investment opportunity

- for capital expenditure

- just in case you see something you want to buy — *spree money*

Saving up money to create a safety net requires a degree of commitment. It is in our nature, after all, to spend rather than to save. But if you can motivate yourself to tuck a little bit away each month I promise you'll never regret it!

## How much is enough?

Just how much savings you should aim to accumulate will be determined by your personal circumstances.

> A single person in his or her twenties without any responsibilities and low overheads probably only needs to have enough cash to cover, say, three months' worth of expenditure.

> A couple with children, a mortgage and a car to run should probably aim to build up as much as six months' expenditure.

If you aren't already lucky enough to have a lump sum available to form your safety net, then the best way to build it up is to establish a pattern of regular saving each week or each month. Remember, something is better than nothing; even if it is a relatively small amount it will soon add up.

## Your savings strategy

To me the big difference between savings and investment is that the former should be kept where you can get your hands on it at short notice whereas the latter can be locked away for a longer period.

If you have, say, six months' worth of expenditure saved up you don't need instant access to all of it. My advice would be to keep about a third where it is readily available and the rest where you can access it by giving notice. This strategy will allow you to earn extra interest.

Incidentally, if you are in a permanent relationship then ideally you should both have access to the emergency fund. In the event of some problem affecting one of you, the other may need to use this money.

## The options available to you

An emergency fund should meet three basic requirements:

1. It should provide you with total security. Your savings must not be at risk;

2. It must earn as much interest as possible under the circumstances; and

3. It must provide you with the level of access you need.

For these reasons, the number of options available to you is limited pretty much to those listed below:

### Deposit accounts

If you leave money on deposit with a bank, building society or credit union they will pay you interest. How much interest you earn will vary according to:

- How much money you have on deposit; and
- The length of notice you have to give before you can make a withdrawal.

Rates can vary substantially and change all the time. Shop around and don't be afraid to move your money to where it can be earning more for you.

## An Post accounts

An Post offers a good range of savings products, all of which offer above-average returns and some of which are tax-free.

## Membership of a Credit Union

As a member of a credit union you will earn an attractive return on the 'shares' you hold. This return is in the form of a dividend and will vary from year to year and from union to union. However, it is usually well above the rate offered by ordinary deposit accounts.

## Savings and tax

On deposit accounts Deposit Interest Retention Tax (DIRT) is levied on your interest at a standard rate. Even if you are a higher-rate tax payer you won't be liable to pay anything extra. On the other hand, if you are not liable for income tax, over 65 years of age, or permanently incapacitated then you are entitled to claim back any DIRT. You can make a back claim for DIRT tax for up to six years.

## A word about Special Savings Incentive Accounts

These accounts could only be opened between 1 May 2001 and 30 April 2002 and last for five years. The minimum amount you can save in them is €13 a month and the maximum is €254 a month. If you have an account you can increase your savings in it at any time *and for most people this makes sound financial sense.* In addition to earning interest in these accounts, the government will make a €1 contribution for every €4 you save. However, what they give with one hand they take away with the other, since when the account is closed after five years, you have to pay a one-off exit tax of 23% on the interest you have earned.

While the accounts are obviously going to show a good return they aren't going to show a spectacular one. It is possible to close the account early, so if you have one you should consider keeping it part of your emergency fund.

---

*The Money Doctor says ...*

- Saving on a regular basis may not always be easy but it will bring you real peace of mind.

- You should have an emergency fund in place that is sufficient to cover all your bills for between three and six months.

- As with everything, shop around. You could earn a considerably greater return by moving your money to where the best rates are.

- If you have a Special Savings Incentive Account then you should consider saving the maximum amount allowed if you aren't already doing so.

# 15

## THE SCIENCE OF
## BUILDING WEALTH

### PROVEN INVESTMENT TECHNIQUES
### THAT ARE GUARANTEED TO SUCCEED

Every investor faces the same conflict: how to balance risk and reward. Should you accept a lower return in exchange for peace of mind? Or should you attempt to make your money grow more quickly and face the possibility of losses? In fact, the best solution to the dilemma is neither. As this chapter will demonstrate, the optimum way to build up your wealth is to:

- Set clear objectives. Know where you are going and what you want to achieve;
- Diversify. Invest your money in more than one area to combine growth and security;
- Be consistent. Don't chop and change, but stick to your strategy;
- Stay on top of it. Keep an eye on performance all the time; and
- Avoid unnecessary expenses and charges.

In addition to outlining a proven method of making your money grow, this chapter summarises all the major investment vehicles you should consider, providing you with 'insider' tips in relation to:

- Pooled investments.
- Stocks and shares.
- Property.
- Tax-efficient investment.

## Basic investment planning

As discussed in earlier chapters, your *primary* investment priorities should be to:

- Build up an emergency fund;
- Start a pension plan; and
- Buy your own home.

What you should do next will depend on your circumstances.

Whether you have a lump sum to invest or simply plan to save on a regular basis, your objectives will basically revolve around the following questions:

- How much money is involved?
- How long can you tie your money up for?
- What type of return are you looking for?
- What risks are you willing to accept?
- To what extent is tax an issue?

Let's look at each of these in turn.

### *How much money is involved?*

If you are saving regularly then you will have a choice between investing in a specially designed longer-term plan or building up 'blocks' of capital and investing each one somewhere different.

If you have a lump sum, or as you build up 'blocks' of capital, then the choice of investments available to you opens up. For instance, with some capital available, property investment becomes an option, as does buying publicly-quoted shares.

Have a clear idea in your mind of how much you plan to invest and in what form. If you are saving on a regular basis consider how long this will be for. Bear in mind that regular savings products have advantages and disadvantages. On one hand they tie you in and there can be strict penalties for early encashment or withdrawal. On the other hand they force you to be disciplined and take away the tricky decision of how to invest your money. An additional issue to consider is the cost of such plans.

## *How long can you tie your money up for?*

Is there a date by which you need your money back? In other words, are you investing for something specific or just to build your overall wealth?

Investments have varying degrees of accessibility or 'liquidity'. An investment that allows you to get at your money immediately is considered 'highly liquid'. Cash in a deposit account or publicly-quoted shares, for instance, are both liquid. Property and pension plans are not liquid.

How long you stay with any particular investment will partly be determined by the investment vehicle itself (a ten-year savings plan is, unless you break the terms, a ten-year savings plan) and partly by events (there may be a good reason to sell your investment).

## *What type of return are you looking for?*

Returns vary enormously. The graph below shows how €1,000 would have grown over the last 20 years had you invested it in different ways. In summary:

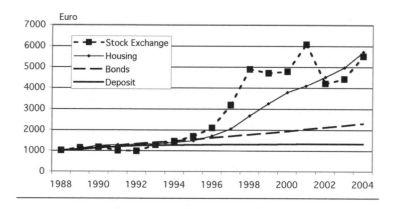

## What risks are you willing to accept?

In general, the higher the return, the greater the risk. The highest possible returns are to be made from investments such as commodities and spread betting, but in both cases you can actually lose substantially more than your original investment. The lowest returns are to be made from investments such as bank deposit accounts and An Post savings plans, where your money can be considered 100% secure.

In formulating your overall investment strategy you need to consider your approach to risk. Are you willing to accept some risk in order to boost your return? How much?

## To what extent is tax an issue?

If you are a higher-rate tax payer, or expect to be, then you need to consider to what extent tax saving is an issue for you.

Bear in mind that there are a number of highly tax-efficient investment options available, though all carry above average risk.

Remember, too, that capital gains are taxed at a much lower level than income, which may make this a more attractive option for you.

## A proven investment strategy

The saying 'don't put all your eggs in one basket' is extremely relevant when it comes to building wealth. In fact, it forms the basis of the only investment strategy I believe can be relied upon: *diversification*. If your investment strategy is too safe, you won't enjoy decent growth. If your investment strategy is too daring, then you risk losing everything you have been working towards. The solution? To diversify your investments so that your money is spread across a range of areas. Which leaves you two simple decisions:

- In which areas should you invest your money?
- How much should you invest in each area?

As already mentioned, you should start by diversifying into the three most important areas of investment: your emergency fund, your pension and buying your own home. Having done this I would suggest putting your money into the following four areas:

1. Pooled investments and bonds;

2. A 'basket' of directly held stocks and shares;

3. Investment property; and

4. Higher-risk and tax-efficient investments such as BES schemes.

Within each area there is much scope for choice, allowing you to vary the amount you invest, the length of your investment, the degree of risk and so forth. You must decide for yourself what mix of investments best suits your needs.

The information below will give you a feel for the various opportunities available. Your next step will depend largely on how active an involvement you want to take. One option is to investigate each area thoroughly yourself. Another option is to allow an authorised professional adviser to handle it all for you. My own suggestion would be to go for a combination of the two. Educate yourself, keep yourself informed, but let an expert guide and support you.

## When long term means long term

One of the biggest mistakes investors make is that they forget their own financial objectives. If you are investing for long-term capital growth — a good, solid gain over, say, twenty years — then if you change your strategy half-way through you must resign yourself to a poor return or even losses. This is true regardless of the investment vehicle you are using.

If a change of strategy is unavoidable then try and give yourself as long as possible to enact it.

There are various areas where investors seem particularly prone to chopping and changing. Long-term savings plans, such as endowments, is one. The stock market is another. In every case (leaving aside some sort of personal financial crisis) the usual reason is despondency over perceived lack of growth or falling values. If you have chosen your investments well, you shouldn't be worrying about the effect of a few lean years or an unexpected dip in values. If you are concerned that you have made a bad investment decision in the first place, do take professional advice before acting. The biggest losses, as we have seen not so long ago, come when an investor panics.

## Pooled investments and bonds

Let me start by saying that I have included several different types of investment in this category:

- Tracker Bonds;
- Unit trusts and other managed funds;
- With-profits funds; and
- Stock Market 'Baskets' (or Guaranteed Stock Market Active Funds).

This is because all of them are what I would describe as 'tailor-made investment vehicles'. That is to say they have been specifically designed to meet the needs of ordinary, private investors. This is in direct contrast to, say, un-tailored opportunities such as buying a publicly-quoted share or an investment property, which aren't aimed at any specific group of investors.

### A few words about pooled investments

Incidentally, a *pooled investment* — sometimes known as an investment fund — is a way for individual investors to diversify without necessarily needing much money. Your money, along with the money of all the other participants, is pooled and then invested. Each pooled investment fund has different, specified objectives. For instance, one might invest in the largest Irish companies, another in UK companies, a third in US gilts and a fourth in Korean property. In each case the fund managers will indicate the type of risk involved. They will also provide you, on a regular basis, with written reports or statements explaining how your money is performing.

Since it would be impossible for all but the richest of private investors to mimic what these pooled investments do, they are an excellent way to spread your risk. A typical fund will be invested in a minimum of fifty companies and will be managed by a professionally qualified expert.

The fund managers make their money from a combination of commission and fees:

- There is often an entry fee of up to 5% of the amount you are investing;
- There will definitely be an annual management fee — usually 1% of the amount invested; and
- If you want to sell your share in a pooled investment you may also be charged a fee.

It is sometimes suggested in the media that fund managers are rewarded too highly. My view is that if a fund is meeting its objectives then it is only fair that the fund managers should recoup their costs and earn a fee for their expertise. I wish journalists would put more effort into reporting performance figures and less on complaining about whether a manager is charging 0.85% a year or 0.93%!

A couple of other points before we look at all the options in a little bit more detail.

1. The funds described below are all medium-to-long-term investment vehicles. In other words, you should be thinking about leaving your money in them for an absolute minimum of five years, and more like ten years or even longer.
2. Although past performance, as it always says in the small print, can be no guide to future performance, *it*

*is still useful to know.* One thing to note is who is making the actual investment decisions and how long they have been doing it for. If the individual manager of a fund has changed recently then the past performance may not be so relevant.

## Unit Trusts

Your money is used to purchase 'units' in an investment fund. The price of the units will vary according to the underlying value of the investments. For instance, if the unit trust specialises in European technology shares then it is the value of the shares it holds which will determine the price of the units. You can sell your units at any time but you should be wary of buying and selling too quickly as charges and fees can eat up your profit.

## Unit-linked Funds

As above, but with the added element of life insurance so that they can be set up and run by life insurance companies.

## Managed Funds

Again these are, in essence, unit trusts. The term is used to denote a fund which makes a wide spread of investments, thus reducing the risk, though you should not assume that this is the case.

## Specialised Funds

A fund that concentrates on a very specific market opportunity, such as oil shares or companies listed in an emerging market. This is obviously riskier but if the underlying investment performs well then you will make above average returns.

## Indexed Funds

A fund that aims to match the overall market performance. For instance, you might have a fund that plans to achieve the same return as the UK's leading one hundred shares (FTSE 100).

## Tracker Bonds

A fund that guarantees to return your initial investment *plus* a return based on a specific stock market index or indices. For example, it might give you all your money back after five years *plus* 80% of any rise in the FTSE 100.

## With-profit Funds

These funds are run by insurance companies and they guarantee a minimum return *plus* extra bonuses according to how the fund has performed over the longer term. These bonuses might be added annually (annual bonus) or when the fund is closed after the agreed period of time (terminal bonus). The terms, conditions, objectives and charges for these funds vary enormously.

## Stock Market 'Baskets'

Investors or their advisers choose a number of stocks, which can range from blue chip shares (main banks, etc.) to downright risky stocks. Depending on how risk-averse you are, a percentage of your 'basket' will be conservative solid choices while the smaller percentage will be a little bit of a gamble. Diversification is the buzz word — the greater the spread or choice of stocks, the softer the fall if there is to be a fall.

## A low-risk, medium-term investment option

For a low-risk, medium-term investment option, consider *guaranteed bonds*. These are offered by a range of financial institutions and offer above-average returns in exchange for you locking your money in for an agreed period. Some offer limited penalty-free withdrawals or provide a regular income for the term of the bond.

## Investing in stocks and shares

Direct investment in the stock market is not for everyone. The risk associated with buying individual shares is obviously much greater than when buying into a diversified portfolio of shares, which is essentially what you are doing with a pooled or investment fund. If the share price goes up, yes, you can make a small fortune. But if the price falls or the market crashes then your shares can become worth a fraction of what you paid for them.

For an investor with limited funds, buying shares is probably not a sensible option. However, once you have started to build your capital wealth you should definitely consider adding individual share holdings to your portfolio of investments:

- Over the longer term the stock market has shown a greater return to investors than any of the alternatives, including property;
- Irish investors are not limited to the Irish stock market but may buy shares anywhere in the world;
- The charges for buying and selling shares have dropped dramatically (as the attached graph clearly demonstrates), making it feasible to buy and sell in much smaller quantities;
- There are excellent sources of advice on which shares to buy and sell;
- Shares have widely varying degrees of risk;
- One of the big advantages of share ownership is that you literally own part of the company itself and its assets; and
- Share ownership should bring you a regular income in the form of dividends *plus* capital appreciation (if the company is doing well).

Private investors have a choice of doing their own research and making their own decisions *or* seeking professional help from a stockbroker. Either way, if you are tempted to start buying and selling, you should arm yourself with as much information as possible. Remember, it is ultimately your decision what happens to your portfolio. You should always keep a close watch on what is happening to any company whose shares you have bought, the sector it operates in and the market as a whole. I would particularly recommend the internet for information purposes.

## Gilts

Gilts is the name given to government stock. Governments over the years use 'stock' (rather like an IOU) to raise money to fund their spending. They offer investors a fixed rate of interest for a set period of time in exchange for the use of their savings. The interest is paid without DIRT being deducted — making them very tax efficient for some non-taxpayers. As interest rates in general fall, government stock tends to rise in value. Gilts are a totally secure and inexpensive way to invest. The returns are usually above average and the cost of buying stock is low, normally a one-off charge of 1%.

## Property

It is easy to understand why so many private investors are attracted to residential and even commercial property:

- Property values have risen dramatically for the last 30 years;
- It is possible to fund up to 90% of the purchase price with inexpensive loans;
- Rental income from property usually covers all the expenses — interest, maintenance, tax and so forth;
- Your investment is in bricks and mortar, something solid, that you can actually see; and
- If you make a gain when you sell the property you will pay substantially less tax, because it is not 'income' but a capital gain and thus taxed at a lower level.

Looking at how property prices have increased over the last 20 years: if you had borrowed €180,000 to buy a €200,000 property some 20 years ago you would have seen your €20,000 deposit turn into €341,200 profit!

Furthermore, in the current climate it is possible to take out interest-only mortgages that ensure your rent more than covers the cost of the loan and other overheads.

Clearly, property prices rise and fall so you would be unwise to assume that this is a one-way bet. If the market does fall you may find it hard to sell the property and take out your money. Also, the supply of property to rent has risen so much that in some areas it is now harder to find and keep tenants.

On the other hand, as the saying goes 'they aren't making any more of it' and as planning restrictions become tighter there is every reason to believe that property will continue to be a highly attractive investment. The golden rule, in my opinion, is to pick a location and type of property that is always easy to rent and easy to sell quickly if necessary.

## MONEY DOCTOR WEALTH CHECK

*Tax treatment of rental income*
Basically, your rental income will be treated the same way as if it was income you had earned by self-employment. You will be allowed all your expenses including:

- Wear and tear on furniture;

- Any charges made by a management company or letting agent;

- Maintenance, repairs, insurance, ground rent, rates and so forth; and

- The cost of any other goods or services you supply to your tenants (such as cleaning).

With regard to relief on interest payable on loans borrowed to purchase, improve or repair a rented property this is allowable except, roughly, from the period between 23 April 1998 and 1 January 2002. If you bought rental property during this period you should seek professional advice or contact the Revenue Commissioners to clarify your position. *Do remember that not all your property expenses will be allowable for tax relief in the year in which they are incurred. For instance, the cost of 'wear and tear' will be spread over several years.*

## Tax-efficient investment options

Financial experts have been heard to comment that 'you should never let the tax-saving tail wag the investment dog'. In other words, you shouldn't invest in anything simply to enjoy the tax savings, but should always consider the underlying value of the opportunity.

When it comes to *property investment* there are a number of tax incentives designed to make certain types of property more attractive. Basically these can be summarised as:

- *Capital allowances* when you buy, repair and improve certain sorts of industrial buildings.
- A range of allowances available to owner occupiers and investors in various urban, town and rural renewal schemes, including *Section 23* and *Section 50* investments.
- It is also possible to get substantial tax rebates by investing in *BES (Business Expansion Scheme) schemes*. These schemes require you to lock into a five-year, higher-risk investment and are only suitable for those with a relatively high income and/or substantial other assets.

*The Money Doctor says ...*

- Don't put all your eggs in one basket. Divide your savings and investments into different parts so that if one area doesn't perform as hoped your overall financial objectives can still be met.

- Remember, the stock market has outperformed all other investments over the long term. You can take advantage of this by investing in a pooled fund such as a unit trust *or* directly in shares.

- You must keep reviewing your investment decisions even if you get a professional to help and advise you.

- Investment is for the long term — anything from five years upwards. Don't allow short-term rises and falls in whatever you have invested in to distract you from your long-term strategy.

**MONEY DOCTOR WEALTH WARNING**

As with everything, if you get professional help make sure that your advisers are unbiased and don't only represent one or two firms. Some so-called experts will sell you their solution without listening to your objectives. Choose an Authorised Advisor as described in Chapter 7.

**MONEY DOCTOR WEALTH CHECK**

*If you want more information about investment options ...*

I regularly update the *www.moneydoctor.ie* web site with details of investment opportunities as well as general advice and information. Or you can always write to me for my free fact sheets.

# 16

## A QUICK GUIDE TO SAVING TAX
### AN EASY-TO-UNDERSTAND AND LOGICAL APPROACH TO CUTTING YOUR TAX BILL

Why pay more tax than you have to? Whatever your income, whether you work for someone else or are self-employed, there are plenty of legitimate ways to reduce the tax you pay.

Effective tax planning requires two things:

- A general understanding of the principles of taxation and how it is possible to organise your affairs in the most tax efficient manner.
- Detailed knowledge of the latest tax rules and opportunities.

This chapter will provide you with proven tax saving strategies. For a detailed and up-to-the-minute list of topical tax tips you should visit my web site — *www.moneydoctor.ie* — or write to me for a current fact sheet.

### Tax as a matter of choice

For the super rich — people wealthy enough to live where they want — tax is largely a matter of personal choice. By spending much of their time in countries with a low or no-tax policy, and with the help of expensive financial advisers, they can keep most of their money to themselves. The rest of us are not so lucky. Not only are we stuck with the Irish tax system, but the cost of getting really top-level tax planning advice is expensive. Nevertheless, there are things to be learnt from those tax-shy millionaires:

- To save tax you have to take an interest in the subject. It is the people who blindly accept whatever they are charged who pay most;
- You sometimes have to make sacrifices in order to save tax. You don't necessarily have to do anything as dramatic as moving abroad. However, you might have to put a bit of time and effort into reorganising your finances; and
- Time spent on tax planning almost always pays off. It is rare to come across someone who can't reduce his or her tax bill — even those on PAYE who may believe it will be impossible.

## A complicated system that needs to be watched

You may have noticed that every year our tax rules change to the benefit of some and the detriment of others. The rules get changed so frequently because the State (or rather our politicians) wish to:

- Raise more money.
- Achieve greater fairness.
- Stop taxpayers from taking advantage of the system.
- Encourage or discourage certain behaviour.
- Reward or penalise certain groups.

The constant changing is both a nuisance and an opportunity. On one hand it is impossible to plan ahead since you never really know what is going to happen to tax rules in the future. On the other hand changes may be to your benefit and/or may produce unforeseen tax advantages that you can exploit. Either way, if you want to keep your tax bill to a bare minimum you need to be aware of the major changes as they happen, not just what happens on Budget Day.

## Formulating a tax saving strategy

There is nothing complicated about developing a tax saving strategy.

1. Draw up a list of all the different types of tax you pay;
2. Rank the taxes in order of cost to you;
3. Concentrate your tax saving efforts on the taxes which cost you most and/or which you have the greatest chance of reducing;
4. Check that you are taking full advantage of all your allowances and exemptions; and
5. Consider what other actions you might take to reduce your liability.

For the majority of people the two biggest taxes they pay will be income tax on their earnings and value-added tax (VAT) on their spending. If you fall into this category you should not be disheartened. While it is hard for a consumer to legitimately avoid VAT without limiting what you buy *even if you are on PAYE* (Pay As You Earn) there should still be plenty of opportunities to reduce your income tax bill.

## Tax checklist

Which taxes are you paying? What is each one costing you? The following checklist will help you assess your position.

*Income tax.* A tax on all your worldwide earnings, whether from employment or some other source (such as investments).

*PRSI* (Pay Related Social Insurance) and the Health Levy: both are effectively another form of income tax.

*Benefits-in-Kind:* Again, income tax on any benefits you enjoy as a result of your employment, such as a company car (PRSI and Health Levy taxes now apply to BIKs as well).

*Capital Gains Tax:* In plain language, a tax on any profit you make when you sell an asset.

*Inheritance and Gift Tax:* Capital acquisitions tax is a tax levied on what you leave when you die and on any gifts you make while you are alive.

*Value Added Tax:* A tax on spending. This is included in the price of most items you buy in the shops.

*Corporation Tax:* A tax on company profits.

## 100 top tax tips

Once you have decided which taxes you want to try and reduce then you should go on line to my web site — *www.moneydoctor.ie* — which contains 100 tax tips. If you haven't got access to the web, write to me at the address shown on page 235 and I'll forward you a hard copy of the relevant fact sheets.

---

**MONEY DOCTOR WEALTH CHECK**

*Are you employed? Do you pay income tax on PAYE?*
Several of the top tax tips you'll find on my web site relate to how employees can slash their PAYE tax bill. It may be much, much simpler than you think.

---

## Get to know the Revenue Commissioners

It is hard not to think of the taxman as the enemy but, in fact, I have always found the Revenue Commissioners extremely helpful when I have approached them for information or advice. At any rate, it is worth remembering the old saying that 'knowledge is power'. If you are self-employed, or own some or all of the company you work for, then it is also worth remembering that

- Nine out of ten taxpayers who find their tax return the subject of a Revenue Commissioners' audit will have been chosen for a specific reason.
- Your past record or some aspect of your tax return are the two most likely reasons to be singled out for an audit; and
- If there is some reason why your tax return is unusual you should provide the Revenue Commissioners with an explanation.

The following actions are likely to result in the taxman singling you out for extra (not necessarily wanted) attention:

- Not earning enough from your business. If it looks like you aren't paying yourself enough the taxman may decide to investigate further;
- Unusual turnover patterns. Unless your business is seasonal the taxman is likely to view sudden changes in turnover as suspicious;
- Discrepancies. If your tax and VAT returns are at variance you could be in trouble. Also if there are other discrepancies in any of your paperwork;
- Incomplete information. If you miss something off your return or your figures don't add up, the taxman may wonder if you have made a mistake by accident ... or on purpose;

- Overseas dealings with known offshore financial centres; and
- Late returns. This makes the Revenue Commissioners wonder if you might have something to hide.

The Revenue Commissioners are very professional and, with sophisticated computer programs to assist them, they are able to analyse tax returns to see if they reflect the general pattern of business in any particular sector. Equally, they are very helpful and the advice they offer is free!

*The Money Doctor says ...*
- This short chapter is designed to provide you with general information on how to save tax.
- The first step must be to identify where the possible savings might come.
- Just because you are on PAYE doesn't mean huge savings aren't open to you.
- If you would like to receive 100 detailed, up-to-the-minute tax tips, then visit my web site — *www.moneydoctor.ie* — or write to me at the address on page 235.

# THE MONEY DOCTOR'S
# JARGON BUSTER

## Accident Insurance

An insurance policy which pays out a lump sum if you suffer an accidental injury. For instance, you might receive €20,000 for the loss of a limb, or €50,000 for the loss of your sight.

## Annuity

A fixed amount of money paid to you as an income for a particular length of time. The length of time may be the rest of your life (life-time annuity) or for a set period (temporary annuity). You buy an annuity using a lump sum of money. Once you've purchased it you cannot get your original capital back, and you are locked in to the income agreed at the outset.

## Annuity Rate

Compares the size of an annuity (in other words how much it will pay you each year) with the size of the lump sum required to buy it.

## APR or Annual Percentage Rate

This is the way in which lenders express the rate of interest and charges they're making. You should always compare annual percentage rates before taking out any loan, and you should bear in mind that there are different ways of calculating the cost of any debt.

## Assets

These are physical items such as land, or intangible items such as goodwill, that are owned by a company or a person.

## Bear Market

The term used to describe a falling stock market.

## Bond

This is a certificate of debt raised by individuals, companies or governments. In other words, a way for these entities to borrow money. It can have a fixed date of repayment or a variable one.

## Bull Market

The opposite of a bear market. This is when a prolonged rise in the stock market occurs.

## Capital

Capital is, in essence, the total resources you have, or the amount you have available to invest, or the amount you originally invest.

## Capital Gains Tax

A tax on the increase in the value of assets during your period of ownership.

## Charge Card

A plastic card enabling a purchase to be charged to an account. It is subject to a limit that must be regularly cleared in full, usually every month.

## Commission

This is a payment to a sales person or adviser, usually based on the value of the sale.

## Compound Growth

The process by which interest-bearing savings mount up.

## Credit Card

A plastic card that gives you credit to an agreed limit. The full amount must be paid within a certain time, or be subject to an interest charge if the cardholder decides to pay only the minimum requirement on the balance.

## Credit Insurance

Sometimes called payment protection insurance. This insurance will cover the monthly cost of a debt for a limited period (usually a year) if you can't work because of illness, injury or unemployment. For instance, you might take out credit insurance to cover your mortgage payments.

## Corporate Bond

A fixed-interest bond raised by a company. See 'Bond' above.

## Critical Illness Insurance

This insurance will pay out a lump sum if you're diagnosed with or suffer from any of a list of life-threatening conditions. For instance, if you have a heart attack or cancer you would receive a pre-agreed amount of money.

## Current Account Mortgage

Also known as a flexible mortgage. A mortgage, like your bank current account, that allows you to vary your monthly payments. By over-paying each month you can save yourself a substantial amount of interest and shorten the length of your mortgage by many years. With some lenders you can also avail of a cheque book to withdraw funds.

## Debit Card

An account-linked card that allows you access to your savings or current account. It does not charge interest but will carry a transaction fee.

## Decreasing Term Insurance

This is a very useful sort of life insurance that pays out a lump sum on the outstanding balance if you die within an agreed term. However, the size of the payout falls as the term progresses and capital (i.e. the original amount borrowed) is being repaid. It is ideal for anyone who wishes to leave money to their dependents to pay off, say, a debt such as a mortgage.

## Depreciation

A loss in value of certain assets such as a car or a machine over time.

## Discount Rate Mortgage

A mortgage whose interest rate is kept at a set percentage below the standard variable mortgage rate for an agreed period. You need to make sure that the difference between the normal and discounted rates of interest is not being added to your outstanding loan, which could dramatically increase the overall cost of your mortgage.

## Dividends

The distribution of part of a company's profits to shareholders. It is the money you earn for investing in a company's shares.

## Emergency Fund

Money you set aside in some reasonably accessible form (such as a bank or building society account) which can be drawn upon in the event of some unforeseen need for funds. Sometimes referred to as 'rainy day money'.

## Endowment Mis-Selling

In the 1980s and 1990s thousands of endowment mortgages were sold with endowment policies that didn't grow in value sufficiently to repay the lump sum borrowed at the end of the mortgage term. In other words, borrowers found themselves unable to pay all their mortgage off. This crisis continues as borrowers who took out endowment mortgages come to the end of their mortgage term.

## Endowment Mortgage

A mortgage where your monthly payments consist entirely of the interest on the amount you've borrowed, whilst the loan itself gets paid off using the proceeds of an endowment insurance policy at the end of a mortgage term.

## Endowment Policy

An investment-type insurance policy which pays out a single amount on a fixed date in the future, usually to repay a mortgage or when the policy holder dies, whichever comes first.

## Equity

Another name for shares in a public company, or the amount of free capital in an asset, e.g. home value €400,000, mortgage €100,000, equity = €300,000.

## Escalation

An automatic and regular increase in pension over successive years, either at a fixed rate or linked to inflation.

## Estate

The assets of a person who has died.

## Financial Adviser

A person or firm offering advice about investments, insurance, mortgages and other financial products. See the note on the IFSRA below.

## Fixed-Rate Mortgage

A mortgage whose interest rate is set at a particular level and does not vary during an initial set period. At the end of the period the rate reverts, usually to the normal variable rate for that lender.

## Flexible Whole-of-Life Insurance

This is a life insurance policy which can be used both to provide a lump sum should you die, and as an investment. It guarantees to pay out *whenever* you die.

## Home Income Plan

A scheme usually set up by an insurance company which offers income to the elderly by releasing some of the value tied up in their homes. This type of facility operates in the UK.

## Home Reversion Scheme

A scheme to provide extra capital or income once you're retired. You sell part of your home but retain the right to live in it until you die (or both you and your husband or wife have died if it's a joint scheme). The amount raised can either be kept as a lump sum or used to buy an annuity.

## Hospital Cash Plan

This policy will pay out a lump sum in specified circumstances, for instance if you have to go into hospital, if you become pregnant, and so forth.

## Increasing Term Insurance

Life insurance where the amount of cover, and the cost, automatically increase during the term either by a set percentage each year or in line with inflation. One of the benefits is that the extra you pay assumes that your state of health is still the same as it was when you originally took out the policy even if, in fact, it has deteriorated.

## Inflation

This is the word used to describe rising prices. At one point we suffered very high levels of inflation in Ireland — prices increased by as much as one-sixth a year. Nowadays, inflation is pretty much under control and down to a very low level. But the risk is always there. Note that when inflation rises, so do interest rates — bad news for anyone borrowing money.

## Interest

Interest is the money charged by a lender to a borrower. It's also the amount of money an investor earns from his or her investments. Here are two short examples: if you borrow €100 and you have to pay an annual interest rate of 20%, that means you have to pay the lender €20 a year. If, on the other hand, you invest €100 and receive interest of 5%, that means that the amount you will receive is €5 a year.

## Interest-only Mortgage

Basically, you only pay interest during the term of the loan but you have the option to pay off lump sums at any time on a variable interest rate or can swap back to a capital-and-interest system at any time during the term.

## Irish Financial Services Regulatory Authority (IFSRA)

The Irish Financial Services Regulatory Authority (IFSRA) is in charge of policing the Irish financial services market — that is to say all the advisers, banks, building societies, credit unions, insurance companies and so forth. The IFSRA took over from the Central Bank of Ireland on 1 May 2003.

## Joint Life Insurance

This is life insurance which covers two people's lives, usually husband and wife, paying out a lump sum when either one or both has died. A 'first death policy' will pay out when one of the people covered has died, whereas a 'last survivor policy' pays out only when both of the people covered have died. This type of life insurance is useful as a way of paying off a mortgage or meeting some other liability. Dual life cover will pay out on both lives upon death, irrespective of who dies first.

## Life Assurance

An insurance policy which pays out a lump sum on the death of the insured.

## Mortgage

A loan secured against the value of your home. A mortgage is essentially a contract between a lender and a borrower. It obliges the lender to make money available to the borrower, and obliges the borrower to repay the loan over a specified period of time at an agreed interest rate.

## Mortgage Payment Protection Insurance

This is a special policy designed to cover your mortgage payments for a limited period — usually not more than two years — if you can't work due to an accident, illness or unemployment.

## Negative Equity

Thankfully we haven't seen much negative equity in Ireland. When an asset, especially a home, falls below the value of the loan (or loans) taken out to buy it, this is referred to as 'negative equity'. In other words, suppose you have a house worth €200,000 and your mortgage is for €220,000. Your negative equity would be €20,000.

## Net Worth

The total value of your assets less your liabilites. You calculate it by adding up the value of all your assets and then deducting the total of all your debts. Supposing you have a house, car, and other possessions worth €150,000 and mortgages and loans to the value of €100,000. Your net worth would then be €50,000 (i.e. €150,000 less €100,000).

## Rate of Return

The amount of money you make from an investment, and it's worked out by adding together any capital appreciation and any income you have received. It's expressed as a percentage. When people refer to the 'real' rate of return, they mean the figure has been adjusted for inflation.

## Re-Mortgaging

The process of repaying one home loan with the proceeds from a new home loan, using the same property as security.

## Renewable Term Insurance

Life insurance which includes a guarantee that you can take out a second term insurance policy at the end of the original term. Your rights will not be affected by any change in your health.

## Repayment Mortgage
A mortgage that has monthly payments to repay both the capital and the interest on the loan over a stated term.

## Secured Loan
A loan that is supported by an asset or guarantee that guarantees repayment of a loan.

## Security
Assets such as title deeds of a property, life policies or share certificates used as support for a loan. The lender has the right to sell the security if the loan is not repaid according to the terms of the mortgage agreement.

## Shares
Shares represent, literally, a share in the ownership of a business. Different types of shares will carry different types of benefits. For instance, some may allow you to vote, others may allow you a share of the company's profits in the form of 'dividends'.

## Surrender Value
The amount of money an endowment policy yields when it's cashed in before reaching maturity.

## Tax Avoidance
Legal tax planning by taking full advantage of the tax laws.

## Tax Evasion
Illegal tax planning — where you are breaking the law. If you get paid in cash for doing some work and don't declare it on your tax form, then you are engaging in tax evasion.

## Term Assurance

A life insurance policy taken out for a fixed period of time which pays out if a person dies before the policy matures.

## Tied Agent

Sales people selling products and services on behalf of one company. Their financial advice is neither impartial nor independent.

## Trust

A trust is a legal entity, like a company, or a person for that matter. It allows assets by one set of people — beneficiaries — to be managed and run by other people — known as trustees. Trusts are a useful way of protecting your loved ones and reducing your tax liability.

## Unit Trust

Investors pool their money into a fund which in turn invests in a number of different companies. It's a good way to spread your risk because it allows you to diversify without having to buy lots and lots of shares.

## Unsecured Loan

A loan that is not supported by an asset to guarantee repayment of the loan.

## Variable Rate Mortgage

A mortgage that permits the lender to adjust its interest rates periodically — generally subject to the changes enacted by the European Central Bank (ECB).

## With Profits Policy

An insurance policy that offers a policy holder a share of any surplus in the insurance company's life insurance and pension business.

# APPENDIX 1

## The Money Doctor's Annual House Budget

| Category | Individual invoices | Totals |
|---|---|---|
| ELECTRICITY | | € |
| HOME HEATING (OIL/GAS) | | € |
| HOME TELECOMS (FIXED/MOBILE) | | € |
| TV LICENCE/CABLE TV | | € |
| HOUSEHOLD INSURANCE | | € |
| CAR INSURANCE / TAX / SERVICE | | € |
| SCHOOL FEES/UNIFORM | | € |
| EXTRA-CURRICULAR SCHOOL COSTS | | € |
| ALARM/SECURITY | | € |
| REPAIRS/CLEANING | | € |
| MEDICAL EXPENSES (incl. dentistry) | | €<br>€ |
| CHRISTMAS EXPENSES | | € |
| MINI BREAKS/HOLIDAYS | | € |
| CLOTHES | | € |
| CLUB SUBSCRIPTIONS | | € |
| OTHER | | € |
| | TOTALS | € |

*When you have totalled your expenditure, divide by 12 and that is the money you have to provide monthly. All other costs (e.g. Capital Expenditure, Loans, Dining Out, Drink, Petrol etc.) must be found outside of this budget.*

# APPENDIX 2

## The Money Doctor's Fact Find

Date: _____

This **Fact Find** contains questions about your financial circumstances. An *adviser* needs to know the answers to these questions in order to get a true and complete financial picture so that recommendations appropriate to your financial needs can be made.

### 1. ABOUT YOU

*Self*

Name/s _____

Address _____

_____

_____

Tel (H) _____ (W) _____

Mobile/Fax _____

Email _____

Date of birth _____ Smoker Y / N

Health status _____

Marital status _____

*Spouse*

Name/s _____

Address _____

Address (contd.) _____

_____

Tel (H) _____ (W) _____

Mobile/Fax _____

Email _____

Date of birth _____ Smoker Y / N

Health status _____

Marital status _____

## 2. YOUR FAMILY

| Children's Names | Date of Birth | School/ College | Educational Fees Plans? |
|---|---|---|---|
| _____ | _____ | _____ | _____ |
| _____ | _____ | _____ | _____ |
| _____ | _____ | _____ | _____ |
| _____ | _____ | _____ | _____ |
| _____ | _____ | _____ | _____ |

**Other Dependents** _____

## 3. YOUR EMPLOYMENT/INCOME

### EMPLOYEE

| | *Self* | *Partner* |
|---|---|---|
| Profession/Trade | _____ | _____ |
| Position | _____ | _____ |

Employer _____ _____

Address _____ _____

 _____ _____

 _____ _____

 _____ _____

Years of Service _____ _____

Salary Per Annum
(gross) € _____ € _____

Annual Bonus
(gross) € _____ € _____

Annual Commission
(gross) € _____ € _____

Annual Overtime
(gross) € _____ € _____

Other Annual Income Description _____ Description _____
(gross) € _____ € _____

Other Annual Income Description _____ Description _____
(gross) € _____ € _____

Net Income Per Wk/Mth € _____ € _____

## PERSONAL BANK ACCOUNT DETAILS

    *Self*   *Partner*

Bank _____ _____

Address _____ _____

 _____ _____

 _____ _____

 _____ _____

Sorting Code         _____    _____

Account Number    _____    _____

## SELF EMPLOYED

|  | *Self* | *Partner* |
|---|---|---|
| Name of Company/Firm | _____ | _____ |
| Address | _____ | _____ |
|  | _____ | _____ |
|  | _____ | _____ |
|  | _____ | _____ |
| Nature of business | _____ | _____ |
| Date established | _____ | _____ |
| Number of Employees | _____ | _____ |
| Percentage of Ownership | _____ | _____ |
| Job Title/Responsibility | _____ | _____ |
| Annual Turnover | _____ | _____ |
| Annual Net Profit | _____ | _____ |
| Annual Salary (gross) | € _____ | € _____ |
| Annual Drawings (gross) | € _____ | € _____ |
| Annual Bonus (gross) | € _____ | € _____ |
| Annual Commission (gross) | € _____ | € _____ |
| Other Annual Income | Description _____ | Description _____ |

(gross)   € _____   € _____

Other Annual Income   Description _____   Description _____
(gross)   € _____   € _____

Net Income Per Wk/Mth   € _____   € _____

Date Of Last Tax Return   _____   _____

Date Of Last Accounts   _____   _____

Tax Owed/Due   € _____   € _____

VAT/PRSI Owed/Due   € _____   € _____

## COMPANY BANK ACCOUNT DETAILS

| | *Self* | *Partner* |
|---|---|---|
| Bank | _____ | _____ |
| Address | _____ | _____ |
| | _____ | _____ |
| | _____ | _____ |
| Sorting Code | _____ | _____ |
| Account Number | _____ | _____ |

## 4. ASSETS/LIABILITIES

**Property** *(N.B. for more than 5 properties, please use Property Portfolio form — www.providence.ie)*

| Address | Current Value € | Loan Borrowings € | Lender | Net Value € | Repayments per Month € | Income € | Net Income € |
|---|---|---|---|---|---|---|---|
| | | | | | | | |
| | | | | | | | |
| | | | | | | | |
| | | | | | | | |
| | | | | | | | |

**Bonds / Investments**

| Provider | Type | Current Value € | Premium € | Frequency | Reference No. |
|---|---|---|---|---|---|
| | | | | | |
| | | | | | |
| | | | | | |

**Equities** (*NB for more than 5 shareholdings, please use Providence form*)

| Share Name | | | | |
|---|---|---|---|---|
| Holding Value € | | | | |

**Cash**

| Institution | | | |
|---|---|---|---|
| Balance € | | | |
| Interest Rate | | | |

**Credit Cards**

| Name of Provider | Name of Card | Current Balance € | Current Limit € |
|---|---|---|---|
| | | | |
| | | | |

**Other Assets/Loans**

| Asset/Loan Description | Institution | Asset Value € | Loan Balance € | Monthly Income € | Monthly Repayment € |
|---|---|---|---|---|---|
|  |  |  |  |  |  |
|  |  |  |  |  |  |
|  |  |  |  |  |  |
|  |  |  |  |  |  |

## 5. INSURANCES/ASSURANCES

**Life Cover**

| Company | Reference No. | Type of Cover | € Covered | Monthly € | Location of Policy |
|---|---|---|---|---|---|
|  |  |  |  |  |  |
|  |  |  |  |  |  |
|  |  |  |  |  |  |

**Health Cover**

| Company | Reference No. | Type | € Covered | Monthly € | Location of Policy |
|---|---|---|---|---|---|
| | | | | | |
| | | | | | |
| | | | | | |

**Pensions**

| Company | Reference No. | Monthly € | Current Value € | Maturity Value € | Location of Policy |
|---|---|---|---|---|---|
| | | | | | |
| | | | | | |
| | | | | | |

**House Insurance**

| Company | Reference No. | Monthly € | Buildings € | Contents € | Location of Policy |
|---------|---------------|-----------|-------------|------------|--------------------|
|         |               |           |             |            |                    |
|         |               |           |             |            |                    |
|         |               |           |             |            |                    |

**Other**

| Company | Reference No. | Type | Monthly € | Location of Policy |
|---------|---------------|------|-----------|--------------------|
|         |               |      |           |                    |
|         |               |      |           |                    |
|         |               |      |           |                    |

## 6. PROFESSIONAL ADVISERS

|  | *Solicitor* | *Accountant* |
|---|---|---|
| Name of Firm | _____ | _____ |
| Address of Firm | _____ | _____ |
|  | _____ | _____ |
|  | _____ | _____ |
|  | _____ | _____ |
|  | _____ | _____ |
| Name of Contact | _____ | _____ |
| Contact Numbers | _____ | _____ |
|  | _____ | _____ |

## 7. WILL

YES?    NO?

Location of Will _____

_____

## 8. COMPLETED BY

Client Signature/s _____

_____

Dated _____

Adviser signature _____

Dated _____

*Additional information:*

_____

_____

_____

_____

_____

_____

_____

_____

_____

_____

_____

_____

_____

_____

_____

_____

_____

_____

_____

_____

# APPENDIX 3

## A Typical 'Terms of Business'

### TERMS OF BUSINESS

Terms of Business sets out the basis on which Providence Finance Services Limited will provide business services to you as an individual private client/s of the Company. Please take a few minutes to read through these and if you have any questions, we will be happy to answer them.

- The full name and address of the firm and communication details are set out on the top and bottom of this document.

- Providence Finance Services Limited is regulated by the Irish Financial Services Regulatory Authority (IFSRA) as an Authorised Advisor and a Mortgage Intermediary and a copy of the firm's Statement of Authorised Status from the IFSRA is attached at Appendix 1.

- The services which the firm is authorised to provide are:
  (a) Advising you in relation to the nature of each of the products set out below and advising you as to which of these products is suitable for your needs;
  (b) Identifying and selecting a suitable product producer; and
  (c) Receiving and transmitting orders on your behalf for products to one or more product producers listed in Appendix 2.

### PRODUCTS

**Life Assurance:**
Providence Finance Services Limited has appointments to act in relation to all life assurance products, including life assurance policies, specified serious illness and other protection type policies, pension policies and Personal Retirement Savings Accounts, savings and investment life assurance policies, tracker bonds and other similar instruments.

Providence Finance Services Limited may receive commission and other payments from the product producer to whom orders are transmitted. Summary details of these payments will be included in a product information document, which you are legally entitled to receive before an application for a product is completed, and full details will be included with your cooling-off letter.

**Non-Life Insurance:**
We currently only have one agency for house buildings and contents insurance through the *Independent Mortgage Advisers Federation* scheme whereby we receive up to 20% of the annual premium. However, we will still give 'best advice' in this category.

**Savings & Investments:**
Providence Finance Services Limited holds an appointment from Anglo Irish Bank plc in relation to its range of notice and fixed-term deposit products. Providence Finance Services Limited is remunerated by Anglo Irish Bank by way of commission on the average balance held on deposit, currently 0.50% per annum. We will also inform you where the best deposit rates are maintained.

**Mortgages:**
A list of the mortgage lenders with whom Providence Finance Services Limited holds agencies is contained in Appendix 2.

Providence Finance Services Limited receives once-off mortgage commissions from lenders at a level of up to 1% of the value of the sum borrowed. In addition it may also receive annual renewal commissions of 0.10% of the outstanding loan balance from AIB plc (they remunerate 0.5% initially on drawdowns of loans).

Where an initial discussion with a client indicates that a mortgage application may be viable, the client will be required to pay an up-front commitment fee of a minimum of €250. This fee is to partially defray the costs incurred by the Providence adviser in terms of time and effort expended in processing the application and is non-refundable if the application is not successful or if the client subsequently decides not to proceed. If the application is successful and leads to a loan being drawn down, the fee will be fully refunded within one month of Providence Finance Services Limited receiving its commission from the lender.

Providence Finance Services Limited may also charge clients a fee, particularly if we arrange a product with a producer with whom we may not hold an appointment in writing. Such a fee for our services will be based on the average level of commissions payable by other product producers for similar types of products. If we do this, we will provide you with a written estimate of this in advance of providing any business services.

- It is the policy of the company to avoid any conflict of interest when providing business services to its clients. However, where any unavoidable conflict may arise, we will advise you of this in writing before proceeding to provide any business service. If you have not been advised of any such conflict you are entitled to assume that none arises.

- Providence Finance Services Limited will, if necessary, exercise its legal rights to receive any payments due to it from clients for business services provided by it, and to be reimbursed for any value obtained by the firm for clients arising from payments by the firm on behalf of clients who subsequently default in any payment due to the firm.

- Should a lender claw back commissions as a result of a loan being repaid within the first three years, Providence Finance Services Limited will reserve the right to bill the client the full amount of the clawback.

- Product producers may withdraw benefits or cover on default of any payments due under any products arranged for your benefit. Details of these provisions will be included in your product terms and conditions.

- Any complaint that you have in relation to the business services provided should be made in writing to the firm outlining the nature of your complaint. Any such complaint will be acknowledged within 14 days. The complaint will be fully investigated by Providence Finance Services Limited and a full response will be provided to you. We will aim to provide this response not later than one month from receipt of your complaint. In the event that you remain dissatisfied with the firm's handling and response to your complaint you are entitled to refer your complaint to the Irish Financial Services Regulatory Authority.

- Providence Finance Services Limited is a member of the Investor Compensation Scheme, which provides certain remedies to eligible clients on default by the firm. The main details of the operation and conditions of the Scheme are attached at Appendix 3. Your legal rights against the firm are not affected by this scheme.

- Providence Finance Services Limited is a member of the Irish Brokers Association, the Professional Insurance Brokers Association, the Life Insurance Association and the Independent Mortgage Advisers Federation.

**NB: These Terms of Business are valid from 1 August 2003 until further notice. For sight of the three Terms of Business appendices, please contact the Administration Manager at the address below:**

*Providence Finance Services Limited*
*Lower Kilmacud Road*
*Stillorgan*
*Co. Dublin*
*Ireland*

*Tel +353 1 278 5555*
*Fax +353 1 278 5556*

*eMail info@providence.ie*
*Web www.providence.ie*

# INDEX

advice *see* help and advice
Allen, Woody 139
annual house budget 219
assessing your own situation 8–9
asset financing and leasing 134
assets and liabilities 42–3
assumptions 44
Authorised Advisor and Mortgage
    Intermediary 82–3, 85

bank or building society deposit,
    interest rates 46
borrowing 68–73
    comparing rates 133
    and compound interest 22–3
    guide to 130–38
    most usual ways of 133–7
    secured and unsecured loans
      132–3
    sensible 130–31
    why rates differ 131–2
    *see also* loans; mortgages
BUPA 142, 147

capital
    difference between capital and
      income 20–21
    how much you will need 47
case histories
    debts 93
    financial planning 38–9, 49–54
    making dreams come true 32–3
    relationship with money 4
Central Bank 80, 85
couples 56–66
    building a joint approach 61–2
    and children 64–5
    dialogue 59–60
    and money problems 56–8
    sharing out the chores 62
    *see also* families
credit cards 136

Credit Union 135

debts
    and being debt-free 90–104
    consolidating 100–101
    eliminating 99–102
    getting out of 96–7
    good and bad 71
    in many disguises 91–2
    paying off 96
    and reasons to become debt-free
      94
    and savings 98–9
    sizing up the problem 90–91
    sniper approach 101–2
    taking stock 97–8
    threats to future freedom 93–4
    true cost of 92–3
Dept of Community, Family and
    Social Affairs 129, 162

Einstein, Albert 21
emergency fund 179–83
Equity Release products 116–18
European Central Bank 115

fact find 220–29
families 34, 56–66
    *see also* couples
financial planning 26–54
    assessment of resources, demands
      and targets 39–40
    assets and liabilities 42–3
    capital needed 47
    complete picture 27–8
    for different phases of life 33–6
    examples 49–54
    help and advice 30
    how to write a money plan 32–55
    inflation 44–5
    interest rates 45–6
    investments 46–7

knowledge of personal finance 11
making assumptions 44
monthly income and outgoings
40–42
objective of 32–3
personal factor 48–9
realistic aims 38–9
what should go into 26–7
financial products 67–75

gearing 23–4
government bonds 46–7

Hall, Alvin 97
help and advice 30, 76–89
free 85–6
intermediaries 88
Money and Budgeting Advice
Services 129
on mortgages 119–20
professional 79–81
questions to ask 86–8
*Terms of Business* booklet 79–80
what is available? 78–9
hire purchase 137
home
buying or renting 122
cost of buying 124–5
in designated areas 126
local authority loans 126
State housing grants 127
*see also* mortgages
house budget, annual 219

inflation 44–5
Institute of Bankers in Ireland 81
insurance 73–4
accident or illness 141, 144
brokers 152
different types of 151–2
home 128, 152–4
importance of 150–51
income protection cover 141, 143
insider tips on 155–6
keeping cost down 148–9
life 142, 144–5

Life Insurance Association (LIA)
81
medical, income and life 139–49
motor 154–5
possessions and other asset
150–56
private medical 142, 147
Professional Insurance Brokers
Association (PIBA) 81
term 145–6
which types of cover? 148
whole-of-life assurance 146–7
interest 20–21
compound 21–3
rates 45–6
investments 46, 46–7, 184
basic planning 185–8
gilts 195–6
graph 187
long-term 189–90
medium-term 194
pooled investments and bonds
190–94
property 125–6, 196–7
proven strategy 188–9
risks 187
stocks and shares 194–5
and tax 187–8, 198
*Investors' Compensation Act* 80
Irish Brokers Association (IBA) 81
Irish Financial Services Regulatory
authority (IFSRA) 79–80, 85,
88
Irish Stock Exchange 81

jargon buster 207–18

loans 68–71
guide to 133–7
interest rates 46
overdrafts 134–5
personal or term 135–6
secured and unsecured 132–3
store cards 136–7
*see also* borrowing; mortgages

money
  attitudes to 3–7
  perfect relationship with 3–15
  taking it slowly 13–14
  taking more interest in 11–12
  thinking positively about 14
Money and Budgeting Advice
    Services 129
money lenders 137
monthly income and outgoings
    40–42
mortgages 107–29
  buying a second property 125–6
  current account 69–70, 116
  endowment 113
  and financial advisers 119–20
  fixed or variable 114–15
  frequently asked questions 121–9
  and gearing 23–4
  Independent Mortgage Advisers
    Federation (IMAF) 81
  interest rates 46, 110–11
  interest-only 114
  and mortgage intermediary 82,
    86
  mortgage tracker 115
  not most expensive purchase
    108–9
  overpayments 118–19
  pension-linked 113–14
  repaying early 127–8
  repayment versus interest-only
    111–13
  and secured loans 134
  and the self-employed 123–4
  and State housing grants 127
  switching 123
  taking advantage of mortgage
    revolution 107–8
  tax relief 125
  throwing out traditional rules
    109–10
  trouble making repayments
    128–9
  see also borrowing; loans

overdrafts 134–5

pensions 157–78
  benefits 176–7
  cost 174–6
  diagrams 159
  directors 170–72
  never too early or late 160–61
  number one priority 157–60
  Pensions Board 162
  Pensions Ombudsman 162
  Personal Retirement Savings
    Accounts (PRSAs) 164–5,
    169–70
  planning 163–4
  in private sector 164–5
  quick guide to schemes 165–9
  for the self-employed 165,
    169–70
  Small Self-Administered Pension
    Schemes (SSAP) 171
  taking stock of where you are
    161–2
  tax relief 172
  what happens to contributions
    173
  what will you need? 162–3
percentages 17–19
Providence Finance Services Limited
    230–33

Qualified Financial Advisers 81

relevance of book xi–xiii
retirement 35–6, 162–3
retirement pensions see pensions

St Vincent de Paul Society 129
savings 179–83
  and debts 98–9
  and investments 71–3
  options 181–2
  Special Savings Incentive
    Accounts 182–3
  and tax 182

self-employment
  and mortgages 123–4
  and pensions 165, 169–70
State housing grants 127
stock market 46–7
store cards 136–7
summaries
  debts 104
  family finance 65–6
  financial advisers 86–8, 89
  financial planning 30–31, 54–5,
      65–6
  financial products 75
  insurance 143, 149, 156
  investments 199
  loans 137–8
  mortgages 115–16, 129
  pensions 162, 177–8
  savings 183
  tax 206
  terminology 25
  your relationship with money 15

tax
  checklist 203–4
  complicated system 202–3
  cutting your bill 83, 201–6
  formulating a tax saving strategy
      203
  and investments 187–8, 198
  as a matter of choice 201–2
  mortgage interest relief 125
  and pension funds 172

and the Revenue Commissioners
    205–6
  and savings 182
  tips 204
  terminology 16–25, 207–18

VHI 142, 147

wealth check
  becoming your own accountant
      12–13
  borrowing 131
  couples 57–8, 60–61, 63
  creating a money plan 28–9
  debts 102–3
  financial objectives 36–8
  financial products 67–8
  how financial institutions make
      their money 84
  making a will 29–30
  rental income 197
  web site 121
wealth warning
  advisers 77–8
  calculators 19
  insurance 144
  investment 199–200
  lenders 95
  pensions 160, 173–4
  tax 204
web site xiv, 121, 204
will, making a 29–30